JESUS'
GREAT
MASTER PLAN
To Rescue Earth And Her Children
from the Spiritual Life

JESUS'
GREAT
MASTER PLAN

To Rescue Earth And Her Children
from the Spiritual Life

J O H N   E N T S U A H

ARPress
ILLUMINATING IDEAS
EMPOWERING VOICES

ARPress
45 Dan Road Suite 5
Canton MA 02021

Hotline: 1(800) 220-7660
Fax: 1(855) 752-6001

Ordering Information:
Quantity sales. Special discounts are available on quantity purchases by corporations, associations, and others. For details, contact the publisher at the address above.

Printed in the United States of America.

ISBN-13:   Paperback   979-8-89356-632-1
                  eBook   979-8-89356-633-8

Library of Congress Control Number: 2024903492

Acknowledgments

TO MY LOVELY WIFE, CHRISTINA—I want to thank you for all your love and support. I also want to thank my children—Amethyst, Zadkiel, and Edna—for being such wonderful children. And, special thanks to my son who helped to type my manuscript.

To my brothers-in-law—George and Joseph Swanzy—thanks for your invaluable support.

To Dr. Rosie Milligan and staff—thank you for the excellent services that you provided me in birthing my vision—this book

Dedication

TO MY GODPARENT, MY HEAVENLY FATHER/MOTHER
GOD. And to my elder brother, Jesus, and to all my brothers and
sisters in heaven, who are earnestly waiting for us to return to our
celestial home.

About the Author

JOHN ENTSUAH WAS BORN IN Ghana, West Africa. He came to the United States in 1974. John has a beautiful wife and is the father of five wonderful children. He has studied religion at Summit University in Malibu, California, where he learned more about the nature of God, Jesus the Christ, the universe and creation, as well as the origin of man.

John has had many occupations including maintenance techni-cian, refrigeration technician, maintenance engineer at Ablestick adhesive plant in Los Angeles, California, electrician on merchant marine ships and U.S. Navy ships, as well as worked on air-condi-tioners and steam boilers.

For 30-plus years, John has had personal, spiritual experiences that have enriched his life and motivated him to research into man's purpose in life. It is these things that have inspired, motivated, and compelled him to write this book. He himself has had to wrestle with who God really is, learn about his relationship with Jesus the Christ, develop an understanding about the nature of the universe and Heaven, and examine man's spiritual fall, as well as how to re-turn to his former state of existence.

John's purpose for writing this book concerns his hope that the reader will develop a Christ-consciousness. He strongly believes that Christ-consciousness is the only hope for the human race.

Table of Contents

Preface

Christ Consciousness Is the Only Hope for the Human Race

THE CHRIST CONSCIOUSNESS IS THE key that opens heaven's gate for you to enter.

THE CHRIST CONSCIOUSNESS is the rock upon which the kingdom of heaven is built.

THE CHRIST CONSCIOUSNESS is what brings you to the presence of God and gives you eternal life. CHRIST CONSCIOUSNESS is the bridge that connects the physical universe, as well as the spiritual universe together to create glory.

THE CHRIST CONSCIOUSNESS is what connects you to God directly with-out interference.

THE CHRIST CONSCIOUSNESS gives you the ability to experience God directly within your heart.

It was through Jesus that the Christ consciousness was able to manifest Himself to the world, "And the word was made flesh and dwelt among us." By awakening the Christ consciousness in your heart, sin, disease, and death will vanish from your life and set you free; this was the message of Jesus the Christ. Each and every person is equipped with his or her own separate Christ consciousness that has to be awakened like an engine in every car that has to be turned on. "Christ in you the Hope of Glory"—the Christ consciousness in you is your only hope that will bring you to the glory of heaven and the presence of God.

Begin to learn to be in tune with your Christ consciousness now. This is the first spiritual lesson every Christian must learn in order to go through the rapture. For nobody can bypass his Christ con sciousness and go to heaven, not even an ant. "Nobody cometh to the Father but by me," said the Christ consciousness in Jesus. My friend, immortality and eternal life is a serious business, not a concert. One must approach this with sober seriousness, and then one will find eternal joy. Everybody in heaven uses Christ consciousness to run his life, so you see, my friend, without Christ consciousness, one cannot live in heaven and in the presence of God. This is what the Christians especially need to understand. If Jesus had not been able to awaken His Christ consciousness, He would not have been able to go to heaven and do what He did.

Christianity mentions Christ, but often fails to add the *consciousness* to the Christ. The Christ consciousness is what sustains the whole universe in one eternal day; eternal timelessness—no beginning or end.

My fellow Christians, I want you to remember, and remember it well, that we are here to build a civilization, a culture, and a society where everybody uses Christ consciousness to run his life. This is the only way to maintain peace, harmony, and happiness for all eternity. And so the Christ consciousness in Jesus was called the *Prince of Peace, the King of Kings*, and the rock upon which the whole universe was built. Jesus became the embodiment of the awesome powers of the *Holy Christ Consciousness*. You too must become the embodiment of the same thing to live eternally. This is the challenge before the human race, whether to believe or not. We cannot change God's divine plan, because we did not create ourselves or the planet. We have our freewill choice to align ourselves with God's divine plan for eternal happiness, or to refuse and suffer spiritual death.

We, the *Christian Esoteric Movement* are committed to assisting everybody, every church, and every religion for this awakening process. It is our Holy Christ command from the beloved Jesus and our God parent, the supreme council of creation, the design committee of creation, the angelic superintelligent beings of great creative powers, including the beloved Jesus Himself, who leads the way with the entire citizens of heaven for this spiritual awakening.

Again, remember, there is a divine spark in you; it is like the sun within your chest area with rainbow rays around it, and this is the miniature Christ consciousness in you that has to be awakened. You are a rainbow of light energy, living in a physical body. This rainbow of light energy has consciousness called the Christ consciousness.

The physical body is His vehicle of expression, and it is through this physical body that the rainbow of light energy that is Christ consciousness is able to contact the physical world to create, restore, and supply all our needs. Jesus was the greatest example for the hu-man race to emulate. "Take my yoke upon you and learn of me," was said by Jesus. This is what makes us all royal sons and daughters of God, heirs of the heavenly Kingdom.

The physical body is divided into two parts, the inner part and the outer part. The inner part, sometimes called the soul, is attached to the rainbow of light energy called the Spirit of God. The outer part is the natural man with its own separate consciousness called the human consciousness. This makes us beings with a dual con-sciousness, like a car with two gears. The first stage is human con-sciousness; the second stage is our Christ consciousness.

The human race must now shift its mind set from human con-sciousness to Christ consciousness. This was the message of Jesus two thousand years ago for the children of earth. He gave the great-est example to the human race, that the birth of Christ is the birth of our own Christ consciousness. The crucifixion of Jesus is the cruci-fixion of the natural man with his human consciousness and all sins, disease, and death. The resurrection of Christ is the resurrection of our own Christ consciousness and our Christ's body. This Christ consciousness brings us the eternal gospel of the universe, to trans-form our society into a Christ-like society, our culture into a Christ-like culture, and our civilization into a Christ-like civilization. It is a golden age of civilization. The Christ consciousness also brings us celestial science technology. Out of celestial science technology comes the natural sciences and technology which we use to create cars, air-craft, ships, television, computers, and the rest of our human world. Now we have the celestial science and technology to transform our planet into a celestial planet, a heavenly planet to fulfill the admonition of Jesus Christ, "Thy Kingdom come, thy will be done on earth as it is in heaven." Finally, we will be propelled into the Holy Light Universe through the process of ascension, the ascension of Jesus Christ.

Jesus appreciates our love for Him, but also wants us to care for and be aware of our Christ consciousness. The Christ consciousness in us represents "The Light which lighted every man that cometh into the world." Just as every car is equipped with its own internal engine to power it, every man is equipped with his own internal separate spiritual engine within the combustion chamber of the soul. This is our full God power that has been partially shut down, that Jesus comes to turn on for us. Once we realize this, it becomes an internal war within ourselves and nobody else to create an intellec-tual debate or religious war that so often plagues churches today. In order to avoid this we can:

1. Develop a strong bond with Christ through constant attunement with Him.

2. *Establish a deep sense of love for our Christ consciousness.*

3. **Stay in tune with our Christ consciousness daily because it is our connection to Christ and all things holy.**

4. Pray and mediate on a constant basis. In meditation, we are in contact with our Godly half, and all questions can be an-swered and all needs fulfilled. Only then can healing take place. We can then wake up to this and break down our chains of ignorance which we must defeat to establish eternal salva-tion in order to live happily ever after in the presence of our God parent and beloved Jesus.

Introduction

From Human Consciousness
to Christ Consciousness

A CONCEPT CAME TO ME during meditation, that if God or Jesus can open my spiritual eyes and spiritual ears to be able to communicate with Him, then God or Jesus can direct me on what to do to have a better life. My greatest concern was communication with Jesus. This will enable me to ask Him questions and also to learn more about my own spiritual growth and enlightenment — not just reading the Bible and forming my own opinions as to what God thinks. I want a teacher-student relationship, where the student can ask the teacher questions and get answers. Here, the teacher can transfer to the student what he wants the student to be.

The first book He wants me to read is titled: *Aquarian Gospel of Jesus the Christ*, by Levi. The second book is: The Holy Bible, and the third book is: *The Initiate of the Flame*, by Manly Hall.

Aquarian Gospel

In the first book, the author talks about his vision of the Aquarian age as revealed to him by Jesus. Jesus showed him His life, beginning from His childhood through His teenage years into adulthood, including the training He received from His beloved mother Mary in the Jewish temples. When Jesus was twelve, He traveled to the east from temple to temple, learning and teaching, and became the master of energy. He attained His Christhood at the age of thirty. After that, He returned to His native land to begin His ministry. In the East, Jesus traveled among the snowbound mountains, the monasteries of Tibet, and the mystery temples of Egypt, Persia, India, and Greece. In these temples, He walked and talked with the monks, wise men, and seers. He also taught and learned from them to achieve that great mastery of love which can also be called the Christ consciousness. This period covers the eighteen absent years of Jesus Christ, which were not recorded in the Bible—from when He was twelve years old to when He was thirty. Jesus returned to His native land at the age of thirty to begin His ministry, which lasted for over three years. He then made His ascension to heaven, or the high-energy world. In His mission, Jesus introduced the Christ consciousness as the solution, or savior, of the world. With Christ consciousness, Jesus raised the dead, turned water into wine, walked on the sea, and transfigured his body on the mount of transfiguration. With Christ consciousness, Jesus challenged death on the cross and defeated it by resurrection and ascension to heaven.

This book by Levi opened the door for me to discover who Jesus the Christ really is. It shows that everybody on the planet has to go through the training program to achieve his Christ-likeness before he can go to heaven, as laid down or set forth by Jesus Himself. "Nobody cometh to the father but by me." This is the key.

Jesus shows that, with Christ consciousness, you can conquer death, you can heal the sick, and restore harmony and peace on the planet. With Christ consciousness, you can change the conditions on earth completely.

The Holy Bible

READING THE HOLY Bible also had a great influence on me; it taught me about God's dealings with the children of earth through the ancient prophets, Jesus, and His apostles. They expressed love and high moral values for humanity to emulate, to change the conditions on earth for a better world.

Initiate of the Flame

THE AUTHOR TALKS about the great beings like the masters Jesus, Moses, Krishna, the Sublime Buddha, Mohammed, Zoroaster,

Confucius and many others who were all initiates of the flame. From the flame of God they came and to the flame of God they returned as sons of God. From a common source they came, to a common place they have returned.

Manly Hall talks about the sacred mystery of the pyramid and the cup stone, the knights of the Holy Grail, the Ark of the Covenant, the mystery of the alchemist, the sacred city of Shambella, and much more. This reading had a great impact on me and gave me the inner meaning of life.

My Spiritual Experience

I LEARNED THROUGH intuitive direction that prayer and meditation are the greatest tools that our God parent has given us to use to crawl our way back to Him. Meditation is receiving energy from God, while prayer is transmitting energy to God, energy which contains what you want from God.

With this in mind, I devoted much time to prayer and medita-tion, asking Jesus to open my spiritual eyes that I might see Him and my spiritual ears that I might hear Him, so that I might become a better and more perfect instrument for His great and glorious work on earth.

Then one day as I was in a meditative state, I felt a quickening movement in my heart. It was a soft, sweet feeling, and this feeling spread throughout my whole body as if invisible water or energy had poured over my body. It penetrated every core and every cell. It gave me a sweet joy within myself and a sense of inner knowing that my prayers had been fulfilled by the Lord Jesus. The next intuitive di-rection was constant meditation and prayers. Dreams were also constant; every night's sleep was as if I were putting my physical body down and going to another world to receive training. I would wake up in the morning and would know what to do. Sometimes I would know the Psalms to read for the day as my prayer and message from the Lord Jesus.

This meditative intuitive experience taught me that my heart is the teacher and my head is the student. The student must always communicate with the teacher to learn and to practice. It made it clear to me that the heart is the shepherd and the head is the sheep, and that the sheep must always submit to the Shepherd for divine guidance, direction, or protection to be able to reach its destination. This is the basis of my life. It taught me again that my heart is connected to heaven, while my head is connected to earth, and that there must be a direct, open communication between heaven and earth before heaven can change the earth. The communication between the heart and the head is the solution to raise my energy to transform myself to be able to see and hear Jesus, because Jesus is a high-energy being and requires a high energy in my body to be able to see and hear Him openly. Your cells operate on the same principles.

How do I see Him? Your head was created to be a communica-tion system. Inside your head, behind your eyes, is a screen similar to your television screen, which can also receive pictures and music. The two most important things that I felt to do intuitively were constant meditation and prayer, as well as washing my body in the ocean every week. As I continued to meditate and wash, the energy in my heart intensified, that is, it increased and expanded and started to push the darkness out from my body. With my eyes closed, I saw a dark screen behind my eyes begin to clear up and finally become like a television screen. It was as if my head or brain was now in tune with some heavenly broadcasting station and receiving programs which contained my future and the future of earth and humanity. The screen became white and transparent with something like crys-tal liquid water, so clean, like our regular water that we drink. In the center of the screen was a small, white arrow, constantly spinning and creating pictures to show me or give me information and visions of what is to come in my own personal life and the events to come on earth.

I compare this small, white arrow, which is constantly spinning on the screen, with the small arrow on the computer screen. It is interesting to observe that the human brain can function like a tele-vision system capable of communicating with some heavenly station or a divine being like Jesus. In my vision, I saw an American flag, and I saw myself traveling to America by plane. I saw the schools and colleges that I would be attending, the places I would be working, and the religious institutions that I would be joining.

I saw war, which I can now interpret as the Gulf War which former President Bush and his NATO Allies fought with Saddam of Iraq.

In my vision, I saw armed Moslems in face-to-face confronta-tion with the well-armed soldiers of NATO. I saw rockets and bombs flying in the skies in hundreds. I saw tanks and planes, jet fighters, and helicopters. There was a lot of killing and destruction and a great, dark smoke. I can now say for sure that the smoke was caused by the oil wells that were blown up by Saddam in Kuwait.

I saw myself working on a ship and traveling from one country to another. There were other visions pertaining to myself and the planet that I will not discuss here, but I will discuss them at a later time. The most important thing that I want you to understand is that God has the answer to every question, a solution to every problem. All you need to do is to establish your communication link with Him. Communication between heaven and earth is the key to chang-ing the earth into a celestial planet.

Constant meditation and constant washing were the key factors. Through intuitive knowledge and direction, I washed myself con-stantly in the ocean at least once a week, because for some mysteri-ous reason, the ocean water has some cleansing properties that af-fected my body. Combining washing with meditation, I felt really good. I discovered that the cleansing process must take place exter-nally, as well as internally. During meditation, I received energy for internal cleansing, as well as for raising my energy. During washing in the ocean, I received energy from the ocean for external, or bodily cleansing. This quickly revealed to me intuitively why Jesus said "Except a man be born again of water and of the Holy Spirit, he can not enter into the Kingdom of God."

John the Baptist also said, "I baptize with water unto repentance, but he that cometh after me baptizes with the Holy Ghost and with fire." This shows me that water and fire move hand in hand when it comes to cleansing and creativity. John the Baptist came to give you baptism by water for the cleansing of your body to prepare your body. Jesus also came to give you the fire baptism of the heart for internal cleansing to raise your energy in order to remove the darkness and open up your spiritual eyes and ears. He did this so that you might see and hear Him, so that you might be able to communicate with the citizens of heaven, and to receive divine direction for your own personal life, as well as to learn how to teach others to do the same.

Remember that water baptism and fire baptism are constants that you must do every day or every week. You must meditate daily to draw energy from the universal Christ to feed the Christ fire in your heart. You must also wash in the ocean or salt water to cleanse your body every day or every week. This is what I did to achieve this result. There came a time that I felt I had triggered an unknown world within myself that I couldn't get out of. But the divine hand was at work. Even though I was feeling pains in my head, it urged me to keep going because victory and true happiness await me in this life, as well as eternally. This suffering is but a moment, and I should not worry; all will be fine in the future. And now I stand victorious.

In my vision, I saw the colors of the rainbow within myself. The future of humanity and of the planet is bright. But they will never reach the heights without challenge. Ignorance is the enemy that creates misunderstandings, that creates wars and hostilities, and takes away peace. This retards humanity's progress. Knowledge is power that enlightens and gives understanding for humanity's progress and establishes peace.

Therefore, we must open our hearts and minds and be willing to learn new things to discover what the universe is all about and how we fit into the universal plan of God.

In my vision, I saw a rainbow within myself. It is amazing to see that the true nature of who we are is light energy clothed in physical bodies. And this light energy breaks into a spectrum of colors.

This light energy creates the consciousness in us, and out of the consciousness comes the creative concepts of God that want to be expressed through our physical bodies. Our bodies, then, serve as vehicles of expression.

The creative concepts of God are high-energy concepts that ex-ist inside the high-energy consciousness. This consciousness is called Christ consciousness.

The creative concepts that exist inside the Christ consciousness are the celestial science and technology (as previously mentioned), with which the celestial star systems were created and the holy light universe was formed. Out of the same celestial science and technology comes the natural sciences and technology, with which we cre-ate our ships, airplanes, telephones, radios, computers, communication systems, cell phones, and television systems.

Have you wondered why Jesus, a high-energy being with Christ consciousness, was able to walk on the sea? He was using the celestial science and technology which is much more powerful than your natural science and technology.

He used this technology to transfigure His body on the mount of transfiguration. He used it to heal the sick and raise the dead. He used it to defeat death on the cross and make His ascension into the high-energy world.

With celestial science and technology, you can override the natural world of pain, sin, disease, and death, and transform it into a high-energy world of peace, creativity, adventure, love, harmony, beauty and eternal life in the presence of God.

This was the message of Jesus. He wants us to give up our hu-man consciousness for Christ consciousness, which will give us the celestial science and technology to change our world for the better,— a world where love reigns in the heart, a world of beauty and celestial music of peace.

My inner teacher teaches me these things; therefore, I urge you to go within yourself through meditation to connect with your inner teacher to free yourself from the grip of your low-energy human consciousness to achieve the high-energy Christ consciousness now.

God is the author of my life; therefore, I owe to Him strict con-formity to His divine plan for me and for the universe; this is com-mon sense. I need not be persuaded by anybody. Why? Because I have found Him within myself and in my heart; the kingdom of God is within me. What about you? Have you found Him, or do you go to church every Sunday to listen to some pastor and preacher about how nice Jesus, is without learning to connect with Him in your heart through meditation? This is your challenge; you need to conquer to be able to step into the kingdom of God within yourself. Let me ask you this question, do you have to go to church to find the kingdom of God within yourself? As you answer this question, you will find the kingdom of God.

Why do you have to go to church to find a kingdom that you already have within yourself? I do not say that you shouldn't go to church. But your spiritual common sense should tell you where to go to find the kingdom of God, which is within your heart. Meditation is the key. The mind holds the key to the heart. In meditation, you bring your mind in tune with your heart and step into the secret chamber of your heart. Here you will find Christ sitting upon the mercy seat, ready to respond to all your needs. This Christ in your heart is the Godly part of you who is sitting upon the throne of the kingdom of God within you that you need to contact everyday. This is what is missing in the Christian churches today, and it needs to be restored.

There awaits for humanity the next level of consciousness called the Christ consciousness which they must shift in order to bring "Thy kingdom come, thy will be done on earth, as it is in heaven." This is the challenge for humanity today.

We will first journey through the historical records of human consciousness for the past three thousand years on the planet Earth, and then move on to the historical record of the Christ conscious-ness, introduced by Jesus over two thousand years ago to shift humanity's consciousness from human consciousness to Christ con-sciousness. Why? Because humanity fell from the high-energy world of the glory of God, to the low-energy world of humanity today. "All have sinned and have come short of the glory of God," Romans 3:23.

Energy has consciousness; high energy is pure energy and has Christ consciousness, which is the creative consciousness of God. When energy falls from high to low, it becomes impure energy. That is where the difficulties begin. It becomes difficult to create.

Whatever energy we embody in ourselves is what we express physically in our lives, whether in heaven or on earth, because all of life is based upon energy in physical expression.

Our level of energy and consciousness determines who and what we are. Real life begins in the high-energy world where everybody has Christ consciousness, that is to say, high-energy consciousness. This was the message of Jesus over two thousand years ago on earth.

In this high-energy world, creativity goes on with ease, speed, and beauty. Here, everybody has Christ consciousness to create any-thing at all he wants and nobody is denied anything.

Love, beauty, peace, wisdom, harmony, and eternal life reign in their hearts. It is only in the low-energy world where we have disharmony, terrorism, war, and lack of creativity. This is the position of the earth today.

Chapter 1

Jesus' Master Plan to Rescue Earth and Her Children from the Spiritual Fall

JESUS THE CHRIST CAME TO earth to introduce the great master plan to rescue earth and her children from the great spiritual fall. He was to bring them back into the holy light universe, where they have belonged from the beginning as celestial soul children of the most high God.

Christ was the divine spark or the holy Christ consciousness within the secret chamber of every heart that had been shut down and needed to be awakened.

It was a simple master plan designed by the supreme council of creation, the design committee of creation, under the auspices of our God parent, the beloved Jesus Himself, and the entire citizens of heaven.

The Formation of the Great Master Plan

IT WAS ANNOUNCED in heaven and in all the celestial star systems by our God parent that a rescue team had to be sent to earth to rescue it from the great spiritual fall and from the hands of the Luciferians and their anti-Christ consciousness activities.

How Jesus Was Selected

MANY GREAT HOLY light beings applied for this great rescue challenge, and a great conference was held in heaven (Holy Light

1

Universe) by our God parent, the supreme council of creation, the design committee of creation, great beings of great creative powers, wisdom, and love, and all the citizens of heaven including the beloved Jesus and the great archangels. The purpose of this great conference was to formulate a rescue plan to save the earth from the hands of the Luciferians and their anti-Christ consciousness activities, by waking up the divine spark of the holy Christ consciousness within the secret chamber of every heart and in every mind, and in the secret chamber of the heart of the planet Earth to propel humanity and the planet as a unit into the holy light universe to join with the celestial star systems.

Many volunteers were called up to step forward to be examined by our God parent, the supreme council of creation and the design committee of creation, as well as by super intelligent angelic beings of great powers who work in partnership with God.

And the one great being called Jesus was selected to lead this rescue expedition on earth. The rest were given other specific assignments to perform in concert with the plan. Twelve great beings were also selected to form a council to continue the plan on earth after Jesus had awakened the divine spark of the holy Christ consciousness. Other groups of people were also selected to form a nation to start the initial platform; they were known as the children of Israel or the Jewish nation of the tribe of Judah. Read the story of Abraham in the Bible. Within this group is the core group known as the Essene communities, who have all the prophets who will hold direct spiritual communication with heaven to enact the divine plan on earth. They will be the platform and the frontline for the great being Jesus to come in to initiate the awakening of Christ consciousness in the heart of humanity and the planet. It will be done through fire baptism of the heart to reclaim the planet from the hands of the Luciferians and propel the planet back home into the holy light universe, or the glory of God.

The council of twelve will then take the torch of Christ consciousness from Jesus to spread and to lighten the whole planet with the Christ consciousness. Ironically, this plan has not been successful as was expected, given the free choice of humanity.

Humanity has chosen anti-Christ and human consciousness, instead of Christ consciousness, which will give them the celestial science and technology to create heaven on earth, as well as a Christ-like civilization on earth where peace reigns eternally.

The Celestial Science Technologies

JESUS WAS ABLE to demonstrate this technology by transfiguring His body on the mount of transfiguration. He used the same technology to walk on the sea and to calm the ocean. He used it to heal the sick and raise the dead.

It was the awesome power of the holy Christ consciousness in Him that gave Him the ability to challenge sin, disease, and death and to make His resurrection and ascension into the holy light universe.

He gave a perfect example of a total victory, showing humanity that the Christ consciousness is the answer to defeat the Luciferians on the planet. The message was we, the citizens of heaven, challenge you, humanity, by holy Christ's command, to awaken your Christ consciousness to free yourself now and forever.

Among the council of the twelve, there was one great being who we all know as Paul. His assignment was to serve as a bridge to connect the message of Jesus and of Christ consciousness to the gentile world.

Other citizens of heaven will play the role of Holy Spirit. They will be invisible guides to assist humanity to awaken their Christ consciousness, for each and every human being is equipped with his or her own separate Christ consciousness. We all have a divine spark, just like the internal engine in every car. This is the godly part of you who knows everything and has everything you need and can create everything you need for all eternity.

This is a portion of the Creator Himself in you. All that you need to do is to learn to be in tune with Him within your heart through meditation. By so doing, you allow the Christ consciousness to step into your physical life to change the condition of sin, disease, and death, and bring celestial beauty and a Christ-like civilization on earth. A Christ-like civilization is a civilization where everybody uses Christ consciousness to run his or her life, just like your civilization where everybody uses human consciousness to run his life in struggle, hostilities, wars, disease, and death.

It is the consciousness that resides within your heart that determines your life. You are consciousness living in a physical body; never forget this.

It was the Christ consciousness in Jesus that performed the mighty work to show humanity the path to being like Christ and to start the Christ-like civilization to save the earth. This is your destiny, whether you believe it or not. Take it or leave it; the choice is yours.

Those who accept God's divine plan will move forward in spiritual advancement to eternal happiness in the holy light universe and live in the presence of God. The rest will live outside the holy light universe, not in the presence of God, because they do not have the Christ consciousness to connect them to the presence of God. You might call this place outer darkness, the low-energy world or spirit prison. Jesus preached from spirit prison after His death on the cross to awaken the Christ consciousness in those spirit beings that believed in Him in this dimension, and He brought them to the presence of God.

Training of Mother Mary

MOTHER MARY, BORN within the Essene community of the tribes of Israel, had already gone through vigorous spiritual training to prepare her to be the mother of the Christ child.

The Essene community is a group of highly spiritually evolved souls who have direct spiritual communication with heaven. And they are aware of the great plan to rescue earth, and that Christ will be born as the first step in that plan.

The most important lesson is to learn how to bring your head in tune with your heart, how to bring your mind in tune with your heart, and how to step into the secret chamber of your heart and connect with the divine spark of the holy Christ consciousness to receive divine direction pertaining to God's will in everything you do. "Thine will be done on earth as it is in heaven."

Meditation is the key that opens the heavenly gate that mother Mary had to pass on to the Christ child. Meditation is a process where you learn how to be in a receptive mode and how to listen within yourself, how to be in tune with the invisible energies of the holy

Christ consciousness within yourself, as well as the universal Christ consciousness energies.

You learn how to receive and to transmit the holy Christ energy. Meditation is receiving energy; prayer is transmitting energy. It is a two-way communication system, not a one-way communication system.

In meditation, you learn to bring your mind in tune with your internal organs to bless them and heal them and thank them for their good services to you. This gives you a complete mastery over your internal, as well as external self.

Another concept commonly known among the Christian churches is "communion." The true esoteric pronunciation is "come in union."

You are coming in union with the invisible energies of the holy Christ consciousness and absorbing this energy into the secret chamber of your heart to feed the Christ fire, or the divine man-child, to grow bigger and bigger until He reaches His full growth. Mary had to pass all this information to Jesus. All of this is unknown to the average Christian because they don't seek open communication with heaven so they can be taught directly from heaven.

Chapter 2

The Mesopotamian Civilization

IN THE MESOPOTAMIAN CIVILIZATION, THERE was great emphasis on development of skills and forms of social organizations that would help them to survive because they occupied a position of insecurity relative to their enemies or competitors. Therefore, security was their preoccupation. Insecurity also led the Mesopotamians to be highly inventive.

The main purpose of this discussion is to give you a picture of the journey of human consciousness from the past to the present and towards the future Christ consciousness and not to go into greater details of the Mesopotamian life.

You can get further information from the book titled *The Western Heritage*, seventh edition, volume one, 1715. The authors are Donald Kagan, Steven Ozment, and Frank M. Turner.

Greek Civilization

AS THE HUMAN consciousness continued to reign on the planet, it gave rise to the Greek civilization. Greek thought emphasized democracy, philosophy, science, and spiritual development. It's great philosophical thinkers like Plato, Socrates, Thales, Aristotle, and many more laid the foundation of Western intellectual thought.

Plato suggested that the truths of geometry were really memories of the eternal truths, and that the world consisted of eternal forms and ideas. Our life was only a debased reflection or imitation of that world.

Greek physicists were also trying to understand the origin of the universe. Thales believed that water was the original element from which all the others were derived. Anaximander argued that the universe began with a spiritual force, or nons, whose action on matter produced movement and order. These ideas were similar to that of the first cause principle, or the prime mover, a cosmic god who had created all things, maintained them in their order, and was the ultimate source of truth, justice, beauty, and goodness. At this stage, the human consciousness of the Greek civilization was shifting to the positive side of life, which would move human evolution forward in science and in spiritual and social advancement.

As human consciousness continued to grow, it gave rise to Alexander the Great. Alexander the Great quadrupled the world that the Greeks knew.

He overthrew the Persian Empire.
He made conquests from Libya to Afghanistan.
He also created a Greek empire that spread Greek culture throughout the east.
He then conducted a mass marriage between Persian maidens and Greek nobles as part of his plan to create a unified empire.

This period is called the Hellenistic age; it is the mixing of all people of all cultures by Alexander the Great.

During this period there were so many great Hellenistic philosophers. Philosophers asked questions like: How a free man could live in such a world as this?

In the classical Greek period, the answer to such a question had been much easier—a free man was one who lived in accordance with the laws and gods of this city. Now that the cities had lost their independence, the answers had become more complex. Whatever their disagreements, the new Hellenistic Greeks argued that freedom had to be found within the individual.

A wise man could be free even if he was a slave through intuitive discipline.

The Cynics' philosophers believed that freedom comes from dropping out of society and abandoning all family ties and property, which only create crisis in a person's life.

Epicurean philosophers in 341–270 B.C. taught that a wise man spent his life seeking pleasure and avoiding pain. However, these pleasures were not those of the body, they were the pleasures of the cultivated mind at rest from the cares of the world.

The Stoic philosopher Zeno in 335–263 B.C. taught a doctrine that had considerably greater social impact. The Stoics taught that freedom came from being in tune with the cosmic order.

Like other philosophers, the Stoics had a harsh view of dangers in the world. But because this world was a reflection of the cosmic order, it could not be ignored. They believed that once a wise man understood the cosmic order, he could even improve the world around him.

They argued that superior men were responsible for taking power in government. Stoicism became the creed of the ruling elite, but it never appealed to the masses.

There were other negative aspects which brought the Hellenistic Greek civilization down and allowed room for the Roman civilization that will not be discussed here. You can get this information from the *Western Heritage*, seventh edition, volume one, 1715, by Donald Kagan, Steven Ozment, and Frank M. Turner.

Chapter 3

The Rise of the Roman Empire

HUMAN CONSCIOUSNESS CONTINUED TO EXPAND and gave rise to the Roman Empire, where the emphasis was placed on moral values and self-discipline. In the second century B.C., Rome became open to Greek ideas, and Stoic philosophy became very influential in their empire.

Stoic morality calls for:

- "Conformity with your own human nature"
- "Conformity with the divine world order"
- "Self-mastery, temperance, courage, dedication, and universal humanitarianism"
- Pietas—respect for established authority and tradition
- Fide—faithfulness to responsibilities
- Religio—collective names for the common beliefs that bind people together
- Gravitas—sober seriousness, a sober society
- Virtus—or virtue means manliness or courage

The word luxus, from which luxury is derived, means the weed that chokes a crop. Anyone who abandoned himself to luxury and idleness was a threat to society.

The strength of the Roman Empire's army, civil engineers, economy, society, order, and government was very important.

The Roman Civilization laid the groundwork for the Christian dispensation to begin. At this stage, human consciousness had developed to the point where it was ready to comprehend the message of Christ consciousness, which was to be introduced by Jesus the Christ.

Earlier, the Jewish prophets had announced the coming of a messiah who would deliver Israel from its enemies.

According to the Bible, Jesus came with His disciples and preached reformed Judaism to their fellow Jews. Jesus, however, preached the Day of Judgment that would soon come when the wicked would be punished and the righteous would be rewarded. Jesus' message to the Jews was to abandon sin while there was still time.

Jesus' main goal at this point in time was to connect the Christ consciousness with the human consciousness. He would plant the seed of Christ consciousness into the human consciousness so it would eventually grow and transform human consciousness into Christ consciousness.

The first step was to give the apostles the fire baptism of the heart; that means, the awakening of the divine spark of the holy Christ fire in their hearts. Then they would, in turn, awaken the rest of the world through the fire baptism of heart. John the Baptist said, "I baptize with water unto repentance, but he that cometh after me baptizes with the Holy Spirit and with fire," Matthew 3:11. That means Jesus baptizes with the holy Christ fire.

Jesus also said to His apostles, "Go ye therefore and teach all nations, baptizing them in the name of the father and of the son and of the Holy Ghost, teaching them to observe all things whatsoever I have commanded you, for I am with you always, even unto the end of the world," Matthew 28:19.

This then set the stage to jump-start the awakening process to raise humanity's energy and consciousness from low to high, from human consciousness to Christ consciousness.

Chapter 4

The Fall of the Roman Empire

DESPITE THE SUCCESS OF THE Roman Empire, it eventually fell victim to the barbarian invasions, as well as economic and moral decay from within in the third century.

Now the seed of the Christ consciousness had been planted by Jesus and had taken root and was moving behind and guiding the human consciousness to the next level, the Byzantine Empire.

The Byzantine Empire, with its capital in Constantinople, carried on the traditions of Rome and Greek orthodox Christian church or religion. Nearly a thousand years after Rome's fall, the Byzantium Empire, with its capital in Constantinople, was also conquered by Islam and its prophet Mohammad.

At this stage, the human consciousness was going through an evolutionary growth, being guided by the Christ consciousness through a process known as metamorphosis, which means, a process of changing from one form to another.

The prophet Mohammed announced he had a revelation from God. He taught that other men had been prophets for God or Allah, such as Moses and Jesus. He claimed to be the last prophet, the only one to reveal God's complete truth. He taught monotheism and moral values identical to all religions. Mohammed taught straightforward rituals similar to Jewish rituals and emphasized cleanliness and basic values such as courage, charity, hospitality, and love and promised that anyone who died from the faith would immediately go to heaven. These particular moral values were also identical to those of the Christians.

These moral values are the characteristics of Christ consciousness, which were infused into the human consciousness to transform it into Christ consciousness.

The whole historical journey of the human race is a transformation of consciousness from one stage to another; it is a teacher-student relationship. The teacher is the Christ consciousness, and the student is the human consciousness. The graduation day is when the human consciousness has been completely transformed into Christ consciousness. This will quickly open up the universe and the rest of heaven to the human race. They will no longer be human beings, but Christ-like beings, high-energy beings with high consciousness capable of communicating with the rest of the universe or the high-energy world and heaven. This is the destiny of the earth chil-dren as taught by Jesus Christ as being the divine plan of God for earth.

Chapter 5

The Dark Ages

THE DARK AGES WAS THE next stage in the human consciousness' evolutionary journey. During this period, the barbarian kingdoms took possession of the remains of the Roman Empire. This occurred in the fifth century. Learning, culture, and social welfare were taken over by the church; that is, the Christ consciousness used the church as a tool to provide these things.

The barbarians were converted by the church, and the church was the moral authority. The barbarians often corrupted the church. The church often exploited the terror and awe inspired by its supernatural prestige to control the barbarians.

The barbarians could only be intimidated by the wrath of God and the vengeance of the saints. Only fear inspired by a prestigious saint could prevent a nobleman or a king from profaning his church.

Christian mythology was also necessary to introduce Christian faith and moral values into a barbarian society, and only a display of supernatural powers could make an impression on the barbarian mind or consciousness.

Chapter 6

Middle Ages

FROM THE DARK AGES, WE move to the Middle Ages. Amid the confusion, invasion, and civil disorder, a military aristocracy dominated the kingdom of Europe.

Christ consciousness then introduced the Feudal Order. The social divisions of A.D. 1000 divided humanity into bishops, knights, and peasants. Famine, disease, and short life expectancies were the conditions that shaped medieval beliefs, which were a reflection of darkness or low energy, not the high energies of Christ consciousness.

Christ consciousness continued to infuse into the human consciousness. More light emerged through the feudal order, and there arose Middle Age cities and cathedrals. The great churches combined the material and spiritual ambitions of the age.

National monarchies emerged with the new urban middle class while dynastic marriages established centralized monarchies. Christ consciousness followed up with the Renaissance, the age of discovery, 1375 A.D. A new level of awareness opened up the human consciousness to explore new frontiers of knowledge. Europe was possessed by this passion for knowledge. Knowledge is power, which would eliminate some of the darkness of ignorance in the human consciousness.

The next age was the Reformation, 1525 A.D. The voice of Martin Luther gave birth to Protestantism, which shattered the unity of the

Catholic Church. For more than a century, the quarrels of Protestants and Catholics tore Europe apart.

And in the midst of these religious wars, a few cities discovered that tolerance increased their prosperity and peace. Then came the age of Absolution and Social Contract, 1700 A.D. This also created an argument about the legitimate source of political power, divine right versus natural law.

Chapter 7

Modern Age

THE CHALLENGE STILL CONTINUED. THEN came the American Revolution. The British colonists in America created a society that tested enlightenment ideas and resisted restrictions imposed by England. The new Republic of America was founded on the universal freedom of Christ consciousness. That is the reason why America is the most advanced country in the world today, because progress is forward movement and involves testing new enlightenment ideas.

The Industrial Revolution ushered in technology and mass production, which reduced famine and brought in higher standards of living. The Consumer Revolution emerged, which was fueled by coal, public transportation, and new city services.

There were other revolutionary activities, where leaders in the arts, literature, and political theory argued for social justice and national liberation.

During the Age of Nations, great powers co-operated to quell internal revolts and yet, competed to acquire colonies of their own. Public education and mass communications created a new political life and leisure time.

Then peace was taken by the dark forces in the First World War. The old empire crumbled with the rise of fascism and right wing dictatorship in Italy, Spain, and Germany.

In the Second World War, a new tactic was developed. Civilian populations became the targets as the Nazi holocaust exterminated millions of people.

In the Cold War that followed, the U.S. and the Soviet Union dominated Europe and confronted each other in Korea.

Europe's Third World countries, being burdened with the legacy of imperialism and colonialism, rushed development to catch up with their Western counterparts.

Keeping up with the ever increasing pace of change in science and technology has become the standard of the day. This is the **Technological Revolution**. This change will continue to accelerate until natural science and technology blend with religion and spirituality. The human consciousness blends with Christ consciousness and is transmuted into Christ consciousness, which then will create a godly civilization on earth, which is where real life begins. What should we do with this great knowledge and power after we have acquired them? The answer lies in the creativity and adventure of the holy light universe.

The Future Is Bright!

MODERN MEDICINE, ATOMIC energy, computers, new concepts of time, space, energy, and matter all have a great impact on the life of the human race in the twenty-first century. Their purpose is to push humanity forward in spiritual advancement through body, energy, and consciousness. I would like to repeat this concept for my readers to understand—when the human consciousness blends with the Christ consciousness, it will transmute the human consciousness into Christ consciousness. The result is a Christ-like being, a high-energy body like Jesus, like the Bible says, "And we shall be like Him." When the natural science and technology blend with religion under the Christ consciousness, it will transmute the natural science and technology into celestial science and technology, because a change has occurred from the natural state of existence to a celestial state. Christ consciousness connects us all together into one unified system, a celestial kingdom containing all celestial forms in the holy light universe. In short, we will all be universal citizens capable of traveling to any part of the universe, like a fish in the ocean that is capable of swimming anywhere in the vast depths. It is an enormous blessing, a blessing beyond the description of the human language. "For eyes have not seen, nor ears heard the things that God has prepared for those who love Him," according to the Bible.

Chapter 8

What Humanity Must Do Now

HUMANITY MUST START NOW TO awaken their Christ consciousness. The planet has already awakened and is accelerating gradually just like a car, shifting through its gears. When the planet shifts into second gear, it will break down everything that is not in accordance with the great master plan of the Christ consciousness. Why? Because humanity and the planet are shifting from the low-energy world life to a high-energy world life, and high-energy bodies and consciousness are required to live in a high-energy world among the stars.

The signs of changes on the earth are self-evident today. We witness these changes through the weather, earthquakes, hurricanes, and other ecological disturbances. These trends will continue until the earth reaches its radiance and its final destination.

When Jesus defeated death, it was through the holy Christ consciousness in His actions that gave Him the ability to challenge death and to defeat it on our planet. Without the holy Christ consciousness, all humanity and the planet would die. The Christ consciousness in us and the planet must be awakened to reverse death. The reason why Jesus was sent to earth from the high-energy world was to awaken the earth and humanity through fire baptism of the heart.

Chapter 9

Christ Consciousness Awakening

THE VOICE OF CHRIST CONSCIOUSNESS is an awakening of the Christ consciousness in the entire human race on the planet now.

Just as you have free will to decide what you want to do with your life, the planet also has her own free will to decide what she wants to do with her life.

The planet is a living, breathing being just like you and has decided to move forward into a high-energy world to join with the celestial star system, which is her original habitation, which was also your original habitation before the spiritual fall or energy fall.

To return home is to jump-start the engine within you, which is your heart. Inside your heart is the divine spark of the holy Christ fire called the Christ consciousness. And when the divine fire is awakened, you become aware of it.

Each and every human being is equipped with his or her own separate Christ consciousness from birth by our God parent. That means God put a portion of Himself in our hearts to respond to all our needs before we came into physical life. Is it not written in the Bible that "Your body is the temple of God, that whosoever defiles this temple, him shall God destroy"? 1 Corinthians 6:19

It is also written that "Greater is he who is in you than he who is in the world" 1 John 4:4. "Christ in you, the hope of glory," Colossians 1:27.

All these statements are pointing the way to a divine holy Christ fire within the secret chamber of your heart.

Each and every planet is also equipped with its separate Christ consciousness within the secret chamber of the heart of the planet. Our planet is like a celestial electric bulb with internal filaments that will ignite by celestial electricity, which are the universal invisible energies of the holy Christ consciousness.

The same thing applies to you. You are like an electric bulb with an internal filament in your heart. When the celestial electricity is released into your heart, your heart will ignite and shine through your body like a star or an electric bulb.

Jesus demonstrated this law on the mount of transfiguration; this was the law of energy, vibration, and substance.

He awakened the awesome powers of the holy Christ consciousness within His heart. He used this same law to walk on the sea and also to calm the ocean. And finally, He used the same Christ consciousness to challenge and defeat death on the cross to prove to the world that the Christ consciousness is the solution to humanity's problems.

Connecting With Your Own Internal Powers

YOU WHO ARE ministers, you who are preachers, you who are doctors of religion, we are saying it to you like it is, that unless you learn to bring your mind in tune with your heart and step into the secret chamber of your heart and connect with the divine spark of the holy Christ consciousness, you are wasting your time, for herein lie your powers of eternal life.

Unless you do this, your ministry is a waste of time and your church is a waste of time, for how can you go to heaven without first connecting with your own internal powers? How can an airplane fly without first connecting with its own internal engine?

My fellow Christians, open your hearts and your minds; let your spiritual common sense guide you in your learning process for your spiritual growth and enlightenment.

Be careful with blind faith which leads people to believe and follow wrong doctrines and achieve a false sense of salvation. Do not promote the belief in the worship of the physical flesh of Jesus without teaching the people how to bring their minds in tune with their hearts and step into the secret chamber of their own hearts and connect with the divine spark of the holy Christ consciousness. You cannot connect with Jesus unless you first connect your mind to your heart. Your connection to Jesus and the heavenly world is through your heart.

Folks, this is what is missing in the Christian churches today; they don't have this technical understanding at all. So what are you going to do about this, my friends, ministers, preachers, and doctors of religion?

The kingdom of God lies within your heart, God can be found within your heart, and the divine spark of the holy Christ consciousness can be found in your heart. The divine man-child and the hidden man of the heart can be found in your heart.

Where do you go to find God, the kingdom of God, and the beloved Jesus Christ? You go right straight into your heart by bringing your mind in tune with your heart. This is called meditation.

In meditation, you bring your attention from your mind into your heart to receive divine direction for what should be done. The head and the heart communicate by waves, just like radio waves or cell phone waves.

This is what Jesus, Paul, Peter, James, and John did to show humanity that the gate to heaven is within your heart, not through the wild preaching, pep talks, and crusades. It takes the awakening of the awesome powers of the holy Christ consciousness within your heart to propel you to heaven.

These apostles learned to go directly into their hearts to answer all questions. They did not look through the Bible to answer questions. They did not even quote from the Bible. Why? Because they are always in tune with the Christ in their heart at all times, the Creator Himself who wrote the Bible.

These people never depended upon the intellect of their heads alone; they combined their minds with their hearts together for the heart to direct the mind because the heart knows. The all-knowing God resides inside their hearts.

The heart is the seat of power and the throne room of God within you. By bringing the head and the heart together, you complete the cycle of creative action in your personal life. This is the basis of life that Jesus taught and gave to His apostles to assist in saving the world.

But Christianity had missed the point. They depended mostly upon their heads and not their hearts. They have fallen so deep into the intellect of the mind that the Christ consciousness of the heart is being neglected. And so there are divisions and hostilities among the Christian churches today.

My fellow Christians, the Christ in your heart is your personal God that was born from your God parent, a divine spark of a diamond-shining rainbow.

Your physical body was built around that divine diamond. And for the physical body to communicate with this diamond, it must bring its mind in tune with the heart to establish a communication link to transfer information from the heart to the mind to accomplish a task. Without this, all your life will be a struggle, pain, and suffering because you are going through life alone, with the intellect of the mind, without the help of the Christ consciousness of the heart.

You see, it was the Christ consciousness in Jesus that gave Jesus' physical body the ability to do all those things on earth. Therefore, He became Jesus the Christ. The Christ is the high-energy being that has the creative energy and ability to create. Jesus is the physical body that the Christ used to contact the physical world, just like electricity needs a conductor to transfer energy.

Your spiritual fall was a disconnection from your Christ consciousness within yourself, and Jesus came to assist you to reconnect you to the Christ within your heart through fire baptism of the heart. John said, "I baptized with water unto repentance, but He that cometh after me will baptize you with Holy Spirit and with fire," Matthew 3:11. Without this, all your church programs are a waste of time. The Christ consciousness of the apostles was restored on the day of Pentecost.

The Christ consciousness of the heart uses the mind as the control vehicle; therefore, the mind must submit to the heart and not take matters into its own hands and run the show. The heart is the authority and the commander in chief that commands the mind what to do. Therefore, a communication link between the two is of utmost importance in order to function efficiently enough to create.

Metamorphosis, the Doorway to Heaven

THE WHOLE PLANET and all of humanity is going through the process of metamorphosis. Metamorphosis is defined as a process of changing from one form to another form. Metamorphosis is the tool that God with his Christ consciousness has created to bring about this change of form. Jesus' mission was to awaken the Christ consciousness in the heart of the planet, which had shrunk during the spiritual fall.

After the crucifixion, while His physical body lay in the tomb, His Christ body with His Christ consciousness were working with the divine beings within the secret chamber of the heart of the planet to jump-start, or awaken, and accelerate the divine spark of the holy Christ consciousness to commence the change. He also preached in the spirit world to restore Christ consciousness to those spirit beings that were in prison because they did not awaken their Christ consciousness while in physical life. Being in the spirit prison means these spirits are low-energy spirits; they did not have the high energy of Christ consciousness. They are humans who died, but are living in the spirit world. The Christ consciousness is your full God-created powers that you must have to create your environment and achieve happiness in the internal worlds. Without it, you are doomed forever.

Spiritual Position of the Planet Today

THE DIVINE SPARK of the holy Christ consciousness in the secret chamber of the heart of the planet has grown bigger and brighter ever since Jesus and the great divine beings jump-started it.

Its radiance has now reached about 70 percent; we need another 30 percent to reach the full radiance of 100 percent. The crucifixion and the resurrection cycle of the planet began a long time ago and is accelerating. This is what you see as the earth changes. Earthquakes, hurricanes, storms, climatic changes, and natural disasters of all kinds take place on a planet in its crucifixion stage, or gestation period. They are necessary to give birth to a new planet. This trend will increase as time goes on.

Humanity is asleep and is suffering from what is known as Spiritual, or Christ-like, developmental delay. People do not seem to understand that they should meditate to absorb the divine invisible energies of the universal Christ from the high-energy world, which is being showered on the planet at this moment. It is written in the Bible that, "In the last days I will pour out my spirit upon all flesh, and young men shall see visions and old men shall dream dreams."

This is the time, folks. Open your heart through meditation for the Christ light energy to enter, to start the process of metamorphosis to change you into a Christ-like being. If humanity will not open their hearts for the spirit of God to enter to awaken the divine spark and go through the process of metamorphosis with the planet, then the few who will, will move forward with the planet in spiritual advancement into the holy light universe to join with the celestial star systems.

The rest of humanity will become laggards; they will not be able to complete their spiritual evolutionary growth into Christ-like beings. They will not be able to raise their energy from low to high; they will not be able to live in the high-energy world, which is the presence of God. Energy has consciousness. High energy has Christ consciousness and low energy has anti-Christ consciousness. High energy is the pure energy of love, kindness, and enlightenment. Low energy is the impure energy of hatred, anger, and ignorance. Therefore, high and low energies are opposed to each other in creation, and those humans who are not able to shift from low energy to high energy cannot live in the high-energy world, period.

The Next Stage is the Resurrection of the Planet

AS GOD SHOWERS His high energy on the planet, the planet absorbs this energy to feed the divine spark of the holy Christ consciousness in the heart of the planet. A new high-energy planetary body begins to form around the divine spark to replace the old planetary body. This birthing process is called the resurrection. At this stage, the internal diamond that is the shining new planet is coming out from its old physical shell. The planet begins to break up in natural disasters so that the new planet can resurrect. A new planet is being born through the process of metamorphosis.

This resurrection stage of the planet is referred to in the Bible as the second coming of Christ. But it is you and the planet that must shift from your human consciousness to Christ consciousness level to be able to see and talk with Jesus in His glorified state. It is you who must shift from your level of existence to His level of existence. It is you who must shift from your human-hood to being like Christ by the awakening of the divine spark of the holy Christ consciousness within the secret chamber of your heart. It is not Jesus who needs to come down to your level of existence, your human low-energy world. Jesus is already gone, and He is living in the celestial world, the high-energy world. He wants you to come and join Him in His celestial world above. This is His desire for you. He wants you and the planet to come to His celestial world as a unit, because you and the planet fell as a unit.

Ascension

THE LAST STAGE in Christ consciousness is mass ascension, or the rapture. It is the returning of the shining new planet with its glorified Christ-like beings, or children, to join with the celestial star systems in the holy light universe to meet with our God parent, Jesus, and our celestial brothers and sisters to receive a welcome home.

Chapter 10

Christ Consciousness, the Bridge That Connects All Life in the Universe

JESUS CAME TO EARTH TO introduce Christ consciousness as a bridge to heaven for humanity. He went through the Christ-like developmental stages as a path, a bridge, and a doorway to heaven.

In the first stage, He awakened the divine spark of the holy Christ fire in your heart, also called the fire baptism of the heart.

According to the Bible, Jesus said, "Except a man be born again, he cannot see the kingdom of God. Except a man be born of water and of the Holy Spirit, he cannot enter into the kingdom of God," John 3:3.

The fire baptism of the heart begins the birthing process, as well as builds the bridge to connect you to the kingdom of God.

The second stage is communion—or come in union—with God. You come in union with the universal life force through meditation. Use meditation to connect with the universal fountain, the blood of the universal Christ as fuel to feed the divine Christ fire in your heart. It needs to reach its full growth in order for you to become a Christ-like being. Jesus said, "Unless ye drink my blood and eat my flesh, ye have no part with me," John 6:53.

The blood is the universal life force, fuel, energy, or well springing from the everlasting life, which you must plug in to drink or feed the Christ fire in your heart to maintain your everlasting life. To disconnect yourself from it means death.

The flesh is the Christ body, a new body, a high-energy, glorified body which will form and develop as you continue to drink the blood of Christ, or the universal life force.

The first two stages are the most critical parts of the bridge into your growth in Christ's image; that is, the awakening of the divine spark of the holy Christ fire in your heart and communion, your coming in union with God and the universal life force, the blood of the universal Christ, through meditation. These two have to be established before the rest can follow. The next stages are crucifixion and resurrection.

Now that you have established the two critical parts, as you continue to draw from the universal fountain, fuel, or energy to feed the divine Christ fire in your heart, a new high-energy body is also forming and developing around the holy Christ fire inside of you to replace your natural, low-energy body.

When the new high-energy body reaches its full growth, the low-energy body, the human body, begins to break up. That is the crucifixion stage. When the high-energy body emerges, that is resurrection. This was the message of Jesus Christ to humanity.

As you raise your energy from low to high, you are not dying; you are becoming more alive than ever before.

Crucifixion and resurrection are a shift from your human-hood to becoming like Christ, from a low-energy being to a high-energy, glorified being. You are not dead; you threw away the human body with its low-energy consciousness of pain, suffering, disease, anger, hatred, hostility, wars, and death for a high-energy body of love, compassion, kindness, creativity, peace, beauty, and eternal life to inherit a high-energy world, which is also called the glory of God with Jesus. This is your destiny; take it or leave it.

The last and the final stage is Ascension. The glorified, high-energy, Christ-like being is now returning to His celestial home to meet with His God parent and His celestial brothers and sisters, including the beloved Jesus who has made all this possible through the great master plan He introduced to rescue the earth and humanity.

My beloved friends, let us open our spiritual common sense and have a heart to heart conversation. You see, you fell from a high-energy world to a low-energy world. And now, you must return from the low-energy world to the high-energy world.

The high-energy world is the glory of God or heaven. To live in heaven, you must have Christ consciousness, high-energy conscious-ness, and body.

Nobody can bypass his Christ consciousness and go to heaven. "Nobody cometh to the father but by me," according to John 14:6. Jesus and Christ consciousness are the blueprint that you must look to in order to forge your image in that of Christ's and return to your celestial home.

When your Christ consciousness is awakened in your heart and in your mind, then it becomes active in your life.

The Christ consciousness sets down the rules of how everything works in the holy light universe, as well as in your personal life.

The Christ consciousness within the secret chamber of the heart of the great central sun of the holy light universe is what runs the universe and is the prime mover, the main engine, and draws its source of invisible energy from the great central being that we call God.

The Christ consciousness within the secret chamber of the heart of the great central sun of our galaxy is what runs our galaxy and sustains it.

The Christ consciousness within the secret chamber of the heart of the sun of our solar system is what fills our solar system with light and sustains it.

The Christ consciousness within the secret chamber of the heart of the planet is what runs the planet Earth and sustains it. The Christ consciousness within the secret chamber of our hearts is what sustains our spirits, souls, and our physical bodies. At this moment, it has shrunk to the point of extinction and needs to be awakened by Jesus. This will reconnect us to the universal Christ consciousness, and then we will be able to see Jesus and talk with Him and all the other heavenly beings. For example, when the television power is turned on, it gives the TV the ability to communicate with the main central station to receive programs; the same is true with your Christ consciousness in your heart. This awakening is called the fire baptism of the heart by Jesus. This is what is missing in the Christian churches today.

The Christ Consciousness Has Three Basic Elements

THE FIRST ELEMENT is the physical light for our physical body and the physical life forms. It provides us with light, heat, warmth, physical energy, solar energy, and physical electricity. The second element is the invisible light, or fire, that nourishes and enlightens our souls with the eternal gospel of the universe, or the great master plan of God including love, wisdom, and power. The third element is the divine fire of God, similar to what Moses saw on the mountain.

This third element nourishes our spirit, is self-sustaining or self-generating, and is indestructible. It can only lose its intensity or increase its intensity, it can grow bigger and brighter, or smaller and dimmer. Smaller and dimmer means it is receding, going back to the universal energy, which is its source. If the divine fire of God in you and in the planet diminishes, you and the planet will cease to exist.

That was the reason why Jesus came. The purpose was to reverse this cycle of death by giving you and the planet an energy jump-start in the heart and then accelerate it to the high-energy level to be able to return you and the planet to the high-energy world, heaven.

I would like to repeat this concept again and again to my readers because it's one of the most important parts of my message. And that is, the invisible fire of the holy Christ consciousness is the fuel that you must draw from the universal life force through meditation to feed the Christ fire in your heart and raise your energy from low to high. This is what the Christians are not aware of and are not doing.

Christ consciousness is the bridge that connects us all together on the individual, planetary, solar, galactic, and universal level. It is like a giant ocean that connects all the fish together with the shore, a giant consciousness which occupies the whole cosmic space with all the planets and life forms.

It has high and low levels of consciousness. The ocean represents high consciousness, and the shore represents low consciousness. You and your planet fell from the ocean to the shore, and now you must return to the ocean.

You and your planet disconnected yourselves from the universal Christ consciousness; that is, your Christ consciousness in your heart and in the heart of your planet shrunk to the point of extinction. This was your spiritual fall written about in the Bible over two thousand years ago. And Jesus and his rescue team, the twelve, were sent from the glory of God to earth to awaken the shrinking Christ consciousness in your heart and the heart of the planet to propel you and the planet back home into the holy light universe.

Jesus did not come to the world to die to save the world. Death on the cross is not what saves and pays the price for the sins of humanity. And again, Jesus did not come to earth to die for you but rather, He came to earth to challenge death and to conquer death to show you how you, too, can challenge death and conquer it by awakening the divine spark of the holy Christ consciousness within the secret chamber of your heart and in the heart of the planet.

That was the reason why Jesus said in the Bible, "I come that ye might have life, and that ye might have it more abundantly," John 10:10.

The divine spark of the holy Christ consciousness is life, which was shut down or shrunk, and Jesus came to turn it back on for you so that it might not go out, and you will not die.

Christ consciousness is life, and life is Christ consciousness; therefore, a being that has attained his Christ consciousness has the power to put his body down on the cross and pick it up again. You cannot kill such a being.

That was the reason why Jesus said in the Bible, "I am the resurrection and the life," John 11:25. It was the Christ consciousness speaking through the lips of Jesus. Again, from His own lips He said, "Therefore doth my father love me, because I lay down my life, that I might take it again. No man taketh it from me, but I lay it down of myself. I have the power to lay it down, and I have the power to take it again. This commandment have I received from my father," John 10:17, 18.

How can a being who has power over death sacrifice his life for you, my fellow Christians? You have a misguided understanding of the message of Jesus.

Jesus said, "Nobody cometh to the father but by me." It was the Christ consciousness in Jesus that was speaking—telling humanity that nobody can bypass his Christ consciousness and go to heaven. You must awaken the divine spark of the holy Christ consciousness within your heart first. Christ consciousness is the kingdom of God within you. "Seek ye first the kingdom of God and its righteousness and all things shall be added unto you," John 6:33. ["Seek ye first to awaken the Christ consciousness and its right-use-ness and all things shall be possible to you."]

Jesus brought us life, not death. Stop talking about "He died for you to save you," and start talking about the life He brought us through the awakening of the Christ consciousness within our hearts through meditation and fire baptism of the heart.

Why Humanity Is Still Dying

HUMANITY HAS PARTIALLY disconnected itself from its own Christ consciousness, the mighty God fire in its own heart, which is the power of immortality and eternal life.

Jesus Shows the Way

JESUS CAME TO show the pathway to heaven, a pathway which humanity must pass through to the glory of God to enjoy excitement and eternal life. Jesus said, "Verily, verily, I say unto you—if a man keep my sayings, he shall never see death," John 8:51.

To Live Eternal Life

YOU MUST HAVE eternal body and eternal consciousness, a high-energy body and a high-energy consciousness, and Christ body and Christ consciousness. And this has to be created by God, by His creative consciousness, the universal Christ consciousness through a process known as metamorphosis. Metamorphosis is defined as a process of changing from one form to another form, that is, changing from a low-energy human being with human consciousness to a high-energy, Christ-like being with Christ consciousness.

This was the great master plan introduced on earth by Jesus two thousand years ago. It was a simple plan to create Christ-like beings on earth to inherit the glory of God.

32

The first thing to do is to invite Jesus through meditation to come into your heart to awaken the divine spark of the holy Christ consciousness within the secret chamber of your heart.

The second thing to do is to use meditation to connect and to draw from the invisible fires of the universal Christ consciousness energy, which is the blood of Christ, the universal fountain, and a well springing from everlasting life in the universal space of God, to feed the divine spark in your heart to burn brighter and to grow bigger and bigger until it fills your whole body.

As the divine fire of the holy Christ consciousness is growing in your heart, a new high-energy, glorified body is also forming and growing around it to replace your old low-energy body. Your low-energy body is your human body. That must be crucified for the new, high-energy, glorified Christ body to be resurrected on the resurrection day.

The invisible fire of the holy Christ consciousness that emanates from the great central being (God) that fills the universal space is what Jesus calls His blood, and a well springing from the everlasting life. "Unless ye drink my blood and eat my flesh, ye have no part with me," John 6:53. Unless you absorb or draw this energy to feed the Christ fire within your heart, you cannot become like Him and be part of His kingdom.

As the Christ fire within your heart continues to grow, it finally reaches its full growth and fills your whole body; this then ignites the white fire core within the center of your brain to fire it up to connect you to the universal mind of God. It shows as a halo around your head, while the Christ fire within your heart connects you to the universal heart of God.

You have now found your God connection in your heart and in your mind to complete the circuit of your transformation into a Christ-like being, enabling you to return to your celestial home to meet with your God parent.

As the Christ fire, Christ consciousness, and Christ body in your physical body reach their full growth, this triggers the crucifixion and the resurrection cycle.

Crucifixion or Resurrection

CRUCIFIXION IS THE breaking up the human physical low-energy body for the fully grown high-energy, glorified Christ body with Christ consciousness to come out or rise and this is resurrection.

Again this process is called Metamorphosis of God, the process of changing from one form to another form. Butterflies go through this same process of change, from egg to caterpillar to cocoon to butterfly.

In the case of Jesus, His physical body did not break up. Why? Because He was to convey to humanity that we could bypass the crucifixion, which you call death, to resurrection and ascension.

He proved to us that all these things could be done through the use of the holy Christ fire, or Christ consciousness, in our hearts. Again, I will quote this statement of Jesus, "Verily, verily, I say unto you, if a man keep my saying, he shall never see death."

Now, let us examine this. Our physical body consists of about three billion cells, according to scientists. Each cell has nucleic acid called DNA or has a genetic code of two DNA helix strands, which are the genetic make up of our bodies.

The cells hold energy, liquid energy like your car battery of three cells with liquid sulfuric acid solution with water that produces electricity to provide light and also to start your car engine.

The number of DNA helix strands in the cell is what determines the amount of energy the cell can hold. The DNA helix strands are the heart of the cell. The cell can also be likened to an electric bulb with filaments in it.

The filament is the heart of the bulb; it is a special wire that converts the invisible energy of electricity into physical light. Its capacity to hold more energy wattage depends upon the number of filaments in the bulb.

Jesus was able to increase or grow His DNA strands from two to three and from three to six, and from six to nine, and from nine to twelve, through prayers, meditation, and fasting, and with help from the great archangels, Gabriel and Michael, and the God parent, the supreme council of creation, the design committee of creation who formulated the great master plan to be implemented by Jesus to rescue the earth from a low-energy world to a high-energy world.

Because Jesus increased His DNA helix strands from two to twelve, He was able to draw more energy from His Christ conscious-ness into his physical cells. His physical cells could now hold more than an average human being's two DNA helix strand cells.

Jesus had an enormous amount of spiritual energy stored up in His cells; He now could perform healing by transferring energy to those who needed it.

He could restore life to those whose Christ fire had been shut down in their hearts. That is why he said, "I am the resurrection and the life," John 11:25.

Transfiguration

HE WAS ABLE to transfigure His body because the cells work like electric bulbs that convert the invisible energy of the holy Christ consciousness into physical light similar to the sun of our solar system, just like your electric bulbs that convert the invisible energies of electricity into physical light.

The intensity of the light wattage depends upon the number of filaments in the bulbs. The intensity of the light and energy of the cells depends upon the number of DNA strands in the cells.

Jesus had to develop his DNA strands to twelve to be able to transform the invisible energies of the holy Christ consciousness to become tangible and real on earth. "And the word was made flesh and dwelt among us," John 1:14.

You, too, must be able to grow your DNA strands from two to twelve to be able to bypass the crucifixion to resurrection, and move from death to life.

Jesus was able to walk on the sea because He was able to bring more energy into his physical body cells to lower the density of his body so He became weightless.

Jesus said to His disciples, "Be of good cheer for I have overcome the world." This means that He had achieved mastery over the physi-cal world or concrete material world with His Christ consciousness.

35

And again with His Christ consciousness, He had become the master of energy vibration and substantiation by changing water into wine.

Jesus has total command and control over the internal, as well as the external of His being; this makes Him a Christ-like being. As such, He was able to blend the external, physical body with the internal, high-energy Christ body that has Christ consciousness.

This made Him a physical and spiritual being capable of living in both heaven and on earth, in both the high- and low-energy worlds. That means He has complete mastery over the physical universe, as well as the spiritual universe. "Behold all powers of heaven and earth are given to me," Matthew 28:18. He can live on both heaven and earth at will. He can materialize from heaven, while a being that has not gone through the process of metamorphosis cannot. By this methodology, Jesus has been able to connect the high-energy world to the low-energy world of humanity to raise their energy and consciousness to be able to live in heaven.

This was the blessing that Jesus came to give to humanity and that Christians just don't understand. They think that Jesus came to die to save them, and that they don't have to go through anything. All that they have to do is to believe in Jesus and do nothing, and they will be saved, "Because salvation is by grace, not by works." You are supposed to use meditation to connect with the invisible energy of the universal Christ fire to feed the Christ fire in your heart. This is your work and responsibility; otherwise, you will not make it to heaven.

This is sad news. The followers of Jesus have turned the message of Jesus into concerts and have become great storytellers. Their intellects are overly developed, while the Christ fire in their hearts is starving because they won't use meditation to connect and draw the invisible energy, which Jesus calls His blood, to feed the Christ fire in their own hearts.

God is pouring out His spirit on earth today, but how many Christians are able to tune in and open their hearts to receive this high energy? They are more concerned with the church programs and money, than with the Christ consciousness in their own hearts, which can solve all our problems, including sin, disease, and death.

They are so busy with wild preaching and trying to change the world from the outside in. You so-called pastors and evangelists, you cannot change the world this way.

You change the world from the inside out by awakening the divine spark of the holy Christ consciousness in every heart. This is fire baptism of the heart by Jesus.

It's like when you go into your room and it's dark, and then you turn on your electric light, and the light shines from within the bulb and pushes the darkness away from the room. It then fills the whole room with light. The room is now changed.

If you want to change your life, where do you start? You start with your heart first, by turning on the divine spark in your heart, then your whole body will be filled with light. You then will think and see clearly with no misunderstanding or confusion. Everything will become transparent and visible to you.

Sadly enough, people want to change their heads first, instead of their hearts. That is why the pastors, the evangelists, and preachers have become great intellectuals and great talkers. They want to memorize the whole Bible from page to page, quote by quote, to show their intellectual powers, to change the world from the outside in. That cannot happen. They are wasting their time. The change must start from the heart before it will affect the head.

The heart must teach the head because the heart knows, and the heart is the throne of God. Why don't you go to the heart first to meet with God through meditation and teach others to do the same thing? This God in your heart is called the Christ consciousness, "the Christ in you, the hope of glory."

Mr. Evangelist, Mr. Pastor, stop your wild preaching and begin to teach awakening of Christ consciousness in every heart by Jesus, then the world will change from the inside out.

The beloved Jesus and the ancient apostles did not spend their time quoting from the Bible. They were in constant attunement with God in their own hearts. They were in constant attunement with the holy Christ fire in their own hearts. They were in contact with the holy

Christ consciousness in their own hearts, the part of you that is God and is all-knowing and super intelligent.

It is this God in you that wrote the Bible. They let this God in their hearts speak through their minds and their lips. It was the Christ God in their hearts in action; therefore, they didn't need to memorize the Bible or quote from anything as you do today.

They left this legacy for us to emulate. Start to depend upon the Christ in your heart now, instead of the intellect of your mind, which does not know. Bring your intellect to connect with your heart for action. The Christ consciousness in our hearts connects us all to the heart of the universal Christ consciousness, which contains the eternal gospel and the great master plan of God and the universe.

This is similar to the main data bank of the Internet. Today you have wireless computers which can tune into the Internet's main data bank and retrieve information and download it into the memory bank. All these can be done through radio waves, a form of electric energy frequency that can transmit and receive information. The electric energy is provided by the battery stored up in the heart of the computer in the main communication station, as well as the command center. Without the battery as the heart of the wireless computer, the computer will be useless.

I want you to apply the same principles to yourself. Your Christ consciousness in your heart is like a battery that produces spiritual energy far more powerful than your computer battery, and yet, see what your computer battery does for you?

The Christ consciousness in your heart is a super intelligent light life form capable of connecting you to the heart of the universal Christ consciousness to retrieve information from the grand library of the universe, which contains the great master plan and the eternal gospel of the universe.

This is how I wrote this book; this is how the apostles wrote the New Testament of the Bible.

The universal Christ consciousness also contains celestial science and technology, out of which comes the natural sciences and technology with which you create your cars, ships, airplanes, TV, computers, and so on. The scientists are able to use meditation, which they call imagination, to connect with the universal consciousness to retrieve this scientific and technological information and organize it into a constructive practical use.

The modern Christians are not in tune with their Christ consciousness in their hearts through mediation or imagination. The modern Christians have replaced the Christ consciousness in their own hearts with the paper Bible. Their attention is focused on the Bible. They read and quote from the past; they are living in the past instead of connecting with their own Christ consciousness to give them direct open communication with Jesus and heavenly citizens.

They must come from the past to the present to connect with heaven and Jesus to receive divine direction about what God wants them to say today. Heaven is the teacher and earth is the student. The citizens of heaven are the teachers, and there must be direct, open communication between the students and the teachers. Our God parent will not just stay in heaven and throw a Bible down on earth and say to us, children, just read the Bible and interpret it the way you think is right, and Jesus will come in the last days to carry you to heaven. How would that convey the divine love of our God parent, my fellow Christians? The Bible was given to you as a guideline to assist you to connect with the Christ God within your heart to enable you to communicate with Jesus and heaven in order to receive divine direction in your life.

My fellow Christians, shift your attention from the paper Bible to the Christ consciousness in your heart, the consciousness who wrote the Bible. The Christ consciousness must be awakened in every heart and in every mind by Jesus. When Christ consciousness is awakened, death will be no more; it will be a thing of the past. Life on the planet as we know it today will be no more, and will be replaced by Christ-like beings of transcendent beauty and love. The glorified planet Earth will join with the celestial star systems in the universe. We will then be universal citizens, no longer earth-bound. You will be able to travel to visit other celestial star systems with Christ-like civilization and meet with your celestial brothers and sisters.

Everybody has the creative Christ consciousness to create anything at all he wants according to the grand design of the universal Christ consciousness. This is the great master plan for the beloved earth and her children from the God parent, Jesus, and the supreme council of creation.

Chapter 11

Real Holy Spirit vs. Counterfeit Holy Spirit

SINCE THE INCEPTION OF Christianity and the Church age, there has been a lot of talk about spiritual manifestations of the Holy Spirit in the Christian churches. These manifestations are shrouded in mysteries, so it is very difficult for a person to really understand which spirit is really behind these manifestations—whether it is a high-energy spirit, which is the Holy Spirit, or a low-energy spirit, which is a counterfeit Holy Spirit.

Today in the Christian churches, there are those who profess to have the Holy Spirit speaking through them in strange tongues, which they consider a message from the spirit of God. The question is, who are these Holy Spirits? Where did they come from?

To answer these questions, you must understand that all life began from God, the first cause. The first cause created a universal home for all His created beings and spirit life forms.

The universe is divided into two parts, a high-energy universe, or holy light universe, inhabited by God, divine beings, souls, angelic beings, holy light beings, Holy Spirit, high-energy star systems and planets, and a low-energy universe, which is inhabited by low-energy beings and spirits. These beings and spirits are not holy and are not living in the presence of God. High energy is pure energy, holy energy, and makes a being a holy light being and Holy Spirit.

41

Energy has consciousness; a high energy has high consciousness, pure consciousness, and Christ consciousness. Therefore, all beings that live inside the holy light universe and in the presence of God have Christ consciousness to run their lives.

Low energy has low consciousness, impure consciousness, and anti-Christ consciousness; therefore, all beings that live outside the holy light universe are not in the presence of God and do not have Christ consciousness and are not pure.

The counterfeit Holy Spirit then is a low-energy spirit that lives outside the holy light universe and does not have Christ consciousness to help you, and he speaks strange tongues.

The real Holy Spirit then is a high-energy spirit that lives inside the holy light universe and has the Christ consciousness to assist you to awaken your Christ consciousness in the secret chamber of your heart, also known as the fire baptism of the heart by the Holy Spirit.

The Holy Spirit with Christ consciousness comes to enlighten you about the great master plan for earth and the eternal gospel of the universe, including the celestial science and technology and en-courages you to join with the holy army of Jesus Christ to champion the cause of awakening the Christ consciousness on earth. This isn't just a mere salvation as it is taught by the churches today. Without high energy, a high-energy body, and Christ consciousness, you can-not live in heaven; this is a serious business, not a concert you see in the churches.

The counterfeit Holy Spirit comes from outside the holy light universe and does not have Christ consciousness to live inside the holy light universe or heaven. It does not have the great master plan, the eternal gospel of the universe, nor the celestial science and technology according to the holy Christ design to give you. All that it has is the low-energy destructive forces, lies, and hatred to neutralize the great master plan for earth, so it can then possess the earth as the base for the Luciferians.

Baptism

WHEN YOU ARE baptized with the Holy Spirit, the real Holy Spirit comes in to your heart to awaken the divine spark of the holy Christ consciousness within the secret chamber of your heart; that is, it comes to awaken the sleeping Christ within your heart. The Bible states that "Christ in you is the hope of glory." The awakening helps you to become aware of your own Christ in your own heart to propel you to the glory of God.

This is what the fire baptism of the heart is for, to bring us back into the glory of God from which we fell.

The Counterfeit Holy Spirit

THE COUNTERFEIT HOLY Spirit comes to your head to deceive your mind with lies and makes you speak strange tongues that nobody understands. The counterfeit Holy Spirit shakes your body to create a sensation for everybody to see that you have received the Holy Spirit.

The Real Holy Spirit

THE REAL HOLY Spirit is gentle and makes you feel the sweet joy of the divine spark of the holy Christ consciousness in your heart. The Christ consciousness speaks the universal language and does not need interpretation from anybody.

On the day of Pentecost, when the Holy Spirit with Christ consciousness descended upon the apostles, it gave the apostles the ability to speak tongues. And since the Christ consciousness speaks the universal language, he spoke the language of the people who were there. And there were many tribes with many languages. One apostle spoke the Egyptian language for all Egyptians. Another apostle spoke the Mesopotamian language for all Mesopotamians and so on to convey the message that the Holy Spirit wants to convey from heaven to the people who were there.

If your Holy Spirit cannot speak my language, then your Holy Spirit does not have Christ consciousness; she is a counterfeit Holy Spirit. Tell her to leave you.

It is your divine right to question the Holy Spirit by saying, are you of the Christ consciousness or do you have the Christ consciousness? If she has, she will gladly say yes.

If she is not, she will avoid saying yes by using intellectual con-versation to skirt around it, because this is the area in the spirit world that no spirit can lie about.

Herein lies the power for the Christians to question and examine their Holy Spirit, especially the Pentecostals, Evangelicals, and the fundamental Christians who are so entrenched in the belief that every spirit that talks through them in tongues is the Holy Spirit.

This is the final battle to flush out the Luciferians from the planet. Your sleeping holy Christ fire in your heart has to be awakened now. It is your spiritual war machine to use in order to defeat the counterfeit Holy Spirit, the Luciferians, and the devil. Without this, Christianity is completely powerless before the devil.

Eternal Life

IN ORDER TO HAVE ETERNAL life in the presence of God in the holy light universe, you must have eternal body and eternal consciousness. This has to be created by God with you and His creative consciousness, the universal Christ consciousness.

The Christ consciousness uses a process known as metamorphosis as His creative machine to mold, to create, and to recreate according to the grand design of the great master plan of God.

Metamorphosis is defined as changing from one form to another form. A typical example is how a butterfly changes from egg to caterpillar, to immobilized pupa cocoon, and finally it will break from its cocoon as a beautiful glorified butterfly.

The seed of the butterfly is planted in the egg. The eggs will hatch and the caterpillar will emerge. The caterpillar will feed on the leaves around it to grow into maturity and change into a pupa cocoon and becomes immobilized. Inside the pupa cocoon is where the butterfly is being created by the creative machine of metamorphosis of God.

When the butterfly becomes fully grown, it will break from the pupa cocoon shell and emerge as a beautiful glorified butterfly with a butterfly consciousness endowed with new powers to fly in the sky and from tree to tree and place to place and can go anywhere it wants to.

In the case of the humans, the seed of your eternal life and your eternal body is planted within the secret chamber of your heart by God. The seed has to be awakened through fire baptism of the heart by Jesus. And this was His mission on earth.

Jesus came to awaken the divine spark of the holy Christ consciousness within the secret chamber of your heart to jump-start the creative machine of metamorphosis to create your eternal body with Christ consciousness so you can live in the presence of God and enjoy eternal life.

When the divine spark is awakened in your heart by your call to Jesus, the next step is to use meditation to connect and draw from the invisible fires of the holy Christ consciousness to feed the divine spark in your heart to burn brighter and brighter until it fills your whole body.

The Christ spark in your heart is the essence of God in you, which must be fed in order to grow. Meditation is the process by which you use your mind to be in tune with the invisible fires of the holy Christ consciousness and to draw it into your heart to feed the divine spark. The invisible fires of the holy Christ consciousness that emanate from the great central being (God) and occupy the universal space is the fuel and creative energy that performs the creative action which we call metamorphosis.

Jesus knew that the universal energy is the fuel and blood that keeps everything alive in the universe. To disconnect oneself from it would be a sad mistake. This is what happened to humanity and the planet; this is the spiritual fall which we have taken for granted. And Jesus came to reconnect us, by the awakening of the divine spark in our hearts. Your heart is the heart of God; your heart is the throne room of God. Therefore, whosoever defiles the heart will lose greatly. Never forget this.

After the fire baptism of the heart, the next step is the opening up of the white fire core within the center of our brain called the fire baptism of the head. Your spiritual development starts in your heart, and then continues to your head.

As the holy Christ light in your heart reaches its full growth, it opens up the white fire core within the center of the brain to connect it to the universal mind of God. The divine spark in your heart connects it to the universal heart of God, and reestablishes the broken God connection, which the Bible calls the spiritual fall.

From this time on, your direct spiritual communication system with Jesus and the citizens of heaven is established. You now have access to the eternal gospel of the universe and the great master plan for earth and can join with the holy army of Jesus Christ to assist in the awakening of the holy Christ consciousness in every heart on earth. The Christ consciousness in your heart is your spiritual war machine that has to be awakened to become a holy Christ warrior. Without this, you cannot fight the devil and win.

Christianity and all the mainstream churches are fighting a spiritual war with their lips, and not with the holy Christ fire in their hearts. They do not know how. Come to us and we will teach you how, and then take this learning to your church to teach them.

Chapter 12

Life after Death

LIFE AFTER DEATH HAS BEEN a mystery, even to Christians who profess to know God. If you know God, then why don't you communicate with God in heaven to reveal to you what is behind the veil after death?

Communication with God and heaven then should become the most important thing for humanity to focus their attention on. In order for heaven to change the earth, heaven must communicate with earth openly, and how can you communicate with a being whose spiritual communication system is shut down? The first thing to do is to fix that communication system so vital information can be transferred which will help humanity to change the world.

The first information you'll receive is about the discovery of yourself, the true nature of who you really are, and the many levels of your being. You'll learn about the divine spark in your heart and how to use it. You'll learn where you come from, and what the Creator's purpose is for you.

The second information you'll receive is about God the Creator, His creation, and the eternal master plan for His creation, which is the holy light universe and the holy light beings that inhabit it. You need to align yourself with God's great master plan for your own eternal happiness.

Chapter 13

How Do We Fix or Develop this Communication System with God or Heaven?

FIRST, YOU NEED TO DISCOVER the blueprint, like a mechanic or engineer who wants to fix a defective machine. The first thing he will do is to request the blueprint and the manual of the machine to study its functions and its various parts and determine what they do.

He then will be able to fix the machine because he has a mental picture and working knowledge of it. "Knowledge is power" which will give him the ability to do things which otherwise would be impossible. The same thing applies to you, so let us start now with the Bible since you are more familiar with it.

According to the Bible, your body consists of a physical body, a soul body, and a spirit body. Therefore, you have three body systems which are interconnected to form one whole body.

The Bible left out the most important part. There is a divine spark in the center, or in the hearts, of these three bodies—the essence of God—which serves as the life force that powers up the three body vehicles.

This life force is the engine and the prime mover of the body vehicles. It is an eternal powerhouse for the three bodies. All three bodies must have access to the internal powerhouse to draw energy from it in order to stay alive and be happy.

Your happiness depends upon the intensity of the power and how much access you have over the power. The divine power in the heart can shrink if you do not nurture it through meditation.

When the connecting lines which serve as an energy pathway to the physical body are broken, the physical body dies. You are now left with the soul and the spirit. Your life after death starts here. You have no contact with the physical life like you used to do.

The physical body gives you contact with the physical world. The soul body gives you contact with the soul world. The spirit body gives you contact with the spirit world.

These bodies are vehicles of expression for the God essence within your heart in the various worlds. With the eyes and ears of your spirit, you can see and hear and communicate with the spirit world. With the eyes and ears of your soul, you can see and hear and communicate with the soul world. With the eyes and ears of your physical body, you can see and hear and communicate with the physical world.

All these three communication systems have switches attached to them that can be turned off and on. An electric bulb is a vehicle that can turn the invisible energy of electricity into physical light. Your television set is also a vehicle that can turn the invisible energy of electricity into motion pictures and music.

The electric motor is a vehicle that can turn the invisible energy of electricity into mechanical energy to run a machine. Life, therefore, is God's invisible energy in physical expression.

Life after death, then, depends upon how much access your soul and spirit vehicles have to the eternal powers within the heart. This God power is the kingdom of God within you.

The less access the soul and spirit has to the internal Christ God power in the heart, the more miserable life will be. This power is your full God power that powers up your life at all levels of your being.

If you do not have access at all to the internal powers, then you will be in spirit prison after death. This is your own personal prison and hell, not God's prison and hell. It is a prison and hell caused by your own disconnection from your God source in your heart. In the Bible we read that when Jesus died on the cross, His spirit went to the spirit world to preach to them and give them power. He awakened the divine spark of the holy Christ fire in their hearts, also called the fire baptism of the heart.

You are like a car which cannot connect with its own internal engine and use it. The same thing applies to the majority of Christians today; most of them have no knowledge of this internal power of the heart.

Finally, God is not in the business of creating hell and spirit prisons, as taught by the Christian churches today. A direct communication with heaven will answer all their questions, so they don't need to form their own human opinion about what happens after death.

The most important thing I want you to understand is that your three bodies are built around the central source of power, the holy light energy, or holy light fire, in your heart, by the Creator. It has so many names. This is the God essence in you who wants to express itself in matter, and as such, it needs a vehicle to do that. Otherwise, it will remain invisible and idle, like electricity that is not being used.

The soul, spirit, and physical bodies are its vehicles of expression. It is written in the Bible, "Know ye that your body is the temple of God, that whosoever defiles this temple him shall God destroy." You must understand that the God essence in you needs your temple, just as your temple needs God. This gives purpose and design to life; without those needs and purpose, life will not make sense, life will be idle. God will just be there, doing nothing. Life after death can be exciting or miserable, depending upon how much access your soul and spirit has to the eternal God power in the heart.

Chapter 14

The Mission of Christ and Jesus to Humanity

THE MISSION OF JESUS WAS to come and awaken a planet that had fallen from a high-energy world to a low-energy world. Humanity and the planet fell as a unit; therefore, they must return to the high-energy world as a unit.

What Is a High-energy World?

THE HIGH-ENERGY world is where God lives, also known as the glory of God, heaven. High energy is pure energy. The pure-energy world is also called the Holy light universe. Energy has consciousness—pure consciousness, high consciousness, Christ consciousness, I am that I am consciousness, universal consciousness, and eternal consciousness. High-energy eternal life, high-energy body is a pure-energy body that has no flesh, no blood, and cannot die.

A high-energy being is a pure-energy being that has Christ consciousness and a high-energy body who lives in the presence of God. We sometimes call them Holy Spirits. You must have Christ consciousness and a high-energy body to be able to live in heaven, and Jesus is our example.

Here in this world of high energy, there is peace, creativity, harmony, love, compassion, balance, beauty, and adventure that lead into new frontiers of creative design and learning. Here, you and God are one in creative harmony and peace for all eternity. This is real life.

And you and your planet fell from this high-energy world into the low-energy world. The fall began with one rebellious child, whose name is Lucifer, or Satan. Today, this planet is his base.

What Is a Low-energy World?

WHEN ENERGY FALLS from high to low, things become very difficult. When energy falls from high to low, it becomes impure energy—the opposite of pure energy. Love is pure energy; hatred is impure energy. Therefore, hatred is opposite of love.

Satan, or Lucifer, was once a pure-energy being who fell from high energy to low energy, from the love of God to the hatred of God; therefore, he cannot live in the presence of God or in the high-energy world.

Your planet was once a pure-energy planet in a high-energy world in the presence of God, and all of you had Christ consciousness and divine love. And now you are here in the low-energy world, which is the fall. And you must return to the high-energy world again.

This is where Jesus comes in with the great master plan to jump-start the holy Christ fire in the heart of humanity and the planet to accelerate their energy from low to high.

A low-energy world is a world of low consciousness, impure consciousness, anti-Christ consciousness, human consciousness, hatred, anger, sin, disease, and death—a world of hostility and wars.

It is a world where Lucifer, or Satan, uses low-energy frequency waves to transmit his wicked intentions to those who are in tune with them to create wars, terrorism, and hostility in order to destabilize the planet and humanity to keep them at a low-energy level. Hitler, Osama Bin Laden, and Saddam are examples. The reverse is true that those who are in tune with high energies will bring love, peace, and creativity to the world; examples are Jesus and His apostles and many others, like scientists. Look at what science and technology have done to your world today.

The Voice of Jesus

JESUS INSISTS THAT Christianity and humanity should stop talking about how Jesus suffered for them and died to pay the price for their sins, and that His death on the cross saved them. This is the truth that has been turned upside down by the Luciferians, Satan, and his legions, to defeat the purpose why Jesus came from heaven to earth, from a high-energy world to a low-energy world.

It is carefully designed by the Luciferians to shift the Christians and humanity from the holy Christ consciousness or the holy Christ fire within the secret chamber of their own hearts, to make sure it's completely shut down to keep them at a low-energy level.

The next thing that the Luciferians have done to humanity and Christianity is to focus their attention on the physical flesh of Jesus and not on the Christ consciousness in peoples' hearts. This will keep them powerless and also prevent them from direct, open communication with heaven and Jesus. This is a worship of the physical flesh of Jesus, which will create a false sense of salvation for the Christians and for humanity, although they don't realize it. In this way, the Luciferians are in control of the planet and humanity, and Jesus and God are not.

Jesus especially wants Christians to understand that death on the cross does not save a person. The physical blood that was shed on the cross does not wipe away their sins. Rather, it is the awakening of the awesome powers of the divine spark of the holy Christ conscious-ness within the secret chamber of your heart that will wipe away your sins and save you and give you eternal life. This is what the Luciferians fear the most.

Therefore, make calls to Jesus through meditation to come into your heart to awaken the divine spark of the holy Christ conscious-ness, or holy Christ fire. This is what Jesus wants you to do now. Stop your wild preaching and noise. The time for wild preaching is over.

Now the emphasis is on awakening the divine man-child in your heart, the sleeping Christ in your heart, the hidden man of the heart. Call to Jesus now and open your heart for Him to come in and awaken the sleeping giant through meditation, and then you will find peace and eternal life.

Jesus' Death on the Cross

HIS DEATH ON the cross was a demonstration to show the power of Christ consciousness, that you cannot kill a being who has awakened his Christ consciousness. Such a being has power over death, for Christ is life and life is Christ; therefore, when you, too, awaken your Christ consciousness in your heart, they will not be able to kill you and you will never die.

Then how can you say He died on the cross to save you? How can a being who has power over death sacrifice His life for you? Here at this stage, the Luciferian lies are exposed to set you free.

Call to Jesus to come into your heart now through meditation to turn on your holy Christ fire.

Focus your attention on your heart. Bring your mind in tune with your heart, for your heart is the heart of God; it is the throne room of God. Here is where you meet Jesus with stretched forth arms, saying, come and sup with me.

I am your elder brother. I was not sent by our father to earth to ask my junior brothers to worship me; no, and I say no again. I was sent here by our father to awaken the divine spark of the holy Christ fire within the secret chamber of your heart which had been shut down. This is what is referred to as your spiritual fall in the Bible.

And this was my mission on earth, and you Christians who are supposed to be my people have turned my message into the worship of my physical flesh, wild preaching, and concerts. You see that without the awakening of the Christ consciousness in your heart, you cannot make it to heaven.

I, Jesus, depended upon my Christ consciousness to do the things that I did, and I finally made my ascension. You must awaken and depend upon your Christ consciousness in your heart, for with Christ consciousness in your heart, nothing is impossible to you.

Chapter 15

The Holy Christ Commands

SEEK YE FIRST TO AWAKEN the holy Christ fire within the secret chamber of your heart and all things shall be possible to you.

The holy Christ consciousness in your heart is your hope of glory. All knees shall bow before the holy Christ consciousness in the heart. All must depend upon the holy Christ consciousness to go to heaven. Nobody cometh to the father but by the holy Christ consciousness.

Jesus depended upon the holy Christ consciousness in His heart to raise up the dead, heal the sick, give sight to the blind, change water into wine, walk on the sea, transfigure His body on the mount of transfiguration, challenge death on the cross, and defeat it by resurrection and ascension. This shows that you, too, must depend upon the holy Christ consciousness in your own heart.

The birth of Christ is the birth of your own Christ consciousness. The crucifixion of Jesus is the crucifixion of the natural man with his human consciousness of sin, disease, ignorance, hostility, and death. The resurrection of Christ is the resurrection of your own Christ consciousness. The ascension of Christ is the ascension of your own Christ consciousness. It is the return to your celestial home where your life began, for your life began with God, and to God you must return.

It is a descending and ascending, Alpha, the beginning, the moving out in creation, Omega, the returning to join with Alpha to complete the cycle of creation which makes one celestial day with no beginning and no end before Christ and God.

Realize that the universal life is based upon the principles of Alpha and Omega in balanced action. In the beginning of the creative cycle, God is worshipped as the father, then in the conclusion of the creative cycle, God is worshipped as the mother. The divine mother joins with the divine father to give birth to the divine man-child, the Christ child, the holy Christ fire, the holy Christ consciousness in every heart.

This is where we are at, this moment of earth's creative cycle —where Jesus comes to turn on the holy Christ fire in every heart through fire baptism of the heart.

The divine mother is being suppressed, even in some religious institutions; they say a woman cannot hold the priesthood. If there is a divine father, then there should also be a divine mother to produce divine children. Your spiritual common sense should tell you this.

If there is a masculine priesthood, then there should also be a feminine priesthood to maintain balance of power, harmony, and peace. We must now begin to give recognition to the divine mother to give birth to the Christ child in every heart that is the Christ consciousness; without it, you cannot go to heaven. The message of Jesus was a message of Christ-likeness; it's not just about being saved. And saved as what? As a dog or as a Christ-like being with Christ consciousness like Jesus himself? Salvation without the attainment of Christ consciousness is a false sense of salvation.

Christianity today is so much entrenched in the worship of the physical flesh and blood of Jesus to the point that they miss the spiritual message of Jesus; that is, the inner meaning of everything that He did. The message of Jesus is to awaken the Christ child in every heart of humanity and the planet. This is also called the fire baptism of the heart, which signifies that the birth of Christ has taken place in your heart.

The Christ comes to establish a Christ-like civilization on earth, a civilization where everybody uses Christ body and Christ consciousness to run his life, and not a human body with human consciousness. This is our destiny in the great master plan of Jesus.

Chapter 16

Crucifixion, Resurrection, and Ascension

THE CRUCIFIXION, RESURRECTION, AND ASCENSION as demonstrated by Jesus Christ could be compared to the life cycle of a butterfly.

First of all, let us examine that life cycle. The life cycle of a butterfly consists of four developmental stages: egg, caterpillar, pupa cocoon, and finally, the butterfly. This process of changing from one form to another during this developmental growth is called metamorphosis.

When the female butterfly is ready to lay her eggs, she uses her senses of touch, sight, and smell to find the right spot. This is usually on a plant, the plant the caterpillar will feed on as it grows. She attaches the eggs to a chosen spot with a sticky fluid. Eggs are laid during the warm weather of the growing season.

The egg hatches as dictated by the caterpillar's genetic code. It is also influenced by the environment. In spring, the day gets longer, the weather warms, and the plants start their fresh, new growth. This signals that the caterpillar is preparing to emerge by cutting through its egg shell. This occurs in the mid-season, when there are enough fresh plants to feed on.

It starts to eat the plants and grows. Its body stretches until its skin becomes too tight. The caterpillar stops eating and molts; that is, it sheds its tight skin. Soon it becomes comfortable in a newly formed, looser skin and resumes feeding. Later it will outgrow that skin and molt again. It will go through several molts before it will reach its maturity.

The caterpillar enters the next stage called a pupa cocoon. Once the caterpillar finds a nice suitable place, it transforms into a pupa cocoon, an immobile form protected from the environment. The cocoon is a protective case around itself.

The Final Birth of the Butterfly

IT IS FASCINATING to watch a beautiful, graceful creature emerge from its immobile cocoon shell. It's a miraculous birth by the divine hands. The butterfly pushes and breaks open a hole in the cocoon shell until the shell splits far enough for the butterfly to push its body out.

A minute after emerging, the adult butterfly holds out its limp wings and flaps them slowly. The movement allows blood into the wings' veins, and then it expands the wings to their full length, which allows the wings to stiffen.

Now it is time for the beautiful butterfly to fly from here and there, from flower to flower to drink nectar or water. The butterfly is free at last from its heavy, dense cocoon body which chained it to the ground. Now it's free to fly in the sky to go anywhere it wishes to go.

This is a message from the divine hands to the human race about the metamorphosis that every human being must go through to return to heaven. This relates to the great master plan to rescue earth and humanity, introduced by Jesus Christ over two thousand years ago.

Now let us see how this relates to crucifixion, resurrection, and ascension as a rescue plan.

You see, my fellow Christians, Jesus came to earth from the high-energy world, the glory of God, which was our original home, to give us a rescue plan to apply to return home. But He, as a teacher, must demonstrate the plan in His own personal life to prove it for us to see.

The story begins in the Bible. "You all have sinned and have come short of the glory of God," Romans 3:23. That means you do not have conscious contact with the glory of God anymore.

Your ability to communicate with heaven or with the rest of the universe has been shut down. You are now an isolated planet with human inhabitants who do not have Christ consciousness to communicate directly with heaven.

Therefore, your Christ consciousness has to be awakened in your heart before communication with heaven, or the glory of God, and the universe can be possible.

When the fall occurred, the divine spark of the holy Christ consciousness within the secret chamber of your heart shrank, or shut down, like a television set that has lost its electrical power. Its electrical voltage has now dropped from 120 volts to 3 volts, and it, therefore, does not have enough energy to be able to communicate with the main television station to receive programs. In order for the television to receive programs again, the electrical power for the television set has to be restored.

It was for this reason that Jesus came with a great master plan to restore the Christ consciousness to the human race and the planet. He was like an electrician from heaven, sent to fix and to restore the divine electric power, the divine spark of the holy Christ consciousness in every heart, and also in the secret chamber of the heart of the planet, through fire baptism of the heart. This was His assignment given to Him by our God parent, the supreme council of creation, the design committee of creation, including the angelic super intelligent beings of great creative power and love, and the entire citizens of heaven.

Jesus did not come and ask humanity to worship Him. That was not His interest or His assignment. This is misguided understanding. Jesus is not the only person in heaven or in the universe who cares for the welfare of the children of earth.

Communication with heaven by the churches will remove confusion and misunderstanding and establish unity, harmony, and peace among all the churches, religions, and humanity.

Assignment of Jesus

HE WAS TO descend from heaven to earth to experience the spiritual fall. "For He descended below all things so that He might rise above all things," according to the Bible.

That is, His Christ consciousness within the secret chamber of His heart shut down so that He, too, might experience the spiritual fall and find a way to reawaken it so He could teach us how to reawaken our Christ consciousness also.

Jesus said in the Bible, "I am the way, the truth, and the life; nobody cometh to the father but by Me," John 14:6.

Jesus awakened His Christ consciousness through prayers, meditation, and fasting to communicate with heaven for assistance from the great beings like the archangels Gabriel and Michael, and super intelligent beings of great creative powers, including the God parents themselves, the design committee and the supreme council of creation.

The seed of Christ consciousness, as a divine spark or holy Christ fire, is now awakened in the heart of Jesus. Now He has to feed it with the invisible fires of the holy Christ consciousness from the universal space through meditation. Meditation is receiving energy from God. Meditation is connecting and drawing energy from the universal life force into your heart. This is what Jesus did to conquer death and also to conquer the world. Prayer is transmitting energy to God, which contains the information of what you want God to do for you.

As Jesus continues to feed the divine spark of the holy Christ fire in His heart through meditation, the energy in the heart increases, and a new high energy body with Christ consciousness begins to form and grow around the heart inside His physical body. This is like a butterfly growing and expanding in its cocoon shell.

As the high-energy Christ body with Christ consciousness reached its full growth in the low-energy physical body, the old low-energy physical body began to break up so the high-energy Christ body with Christ consciousness can come out, like a butterfly breaking up its cocoon shell to come out with its new, high-energy, glorified butterfly body and consciousness, with its many powerful capabilities of flying in the sky and from tree to tree. It is no more a caterpillar or cocoon chained down with a heavy dense body. It is now free at last.

This is like the crucifixion and the resurrection. The crucifixion is the breaking up of the old, low-energy, dense, physical body, the natural man with all his sins, disease, and death, for the glorified, diamond-shining Christ body to come out.

The Resurrection is the coming out of the glorified, diamond-shining Christ body with Christ consciousness. You, too, can achieve Christ consciousness and become a new you, a high-energy you, capable of living in heaven and in the celestial star systems, just like a new, glorified butterfly with many powerful capabilities of flying in the sky and from tree to tree.

You are now a universal citizen with all the powers of heaven and earth because you are now a Christ-like being with Christ conscious-ness and a Christ body, or a universal body.

The last stage is the ascension, the returning to your celestial home with your high-energy, diamond-shining, Christ body and Christ consciousness to meet with your God parent and your celestial brothers and sisters to receive a welcome home.

This time, you come to reclaim your heritage.

Chapter 17

Jesus Introduced the Principles of Metamorphosis as the Doorway to Heaven

LET US FOCUS OUR ATTENTION on Jesus to find out more about Him. The great master plan to rescue earth that Jesus introduces from heaven is based upon the principles of metamorphosis.

Metamorphosis is the most powerful tool that God uses for His creative activities to change the natural creation into celestial creation. That means, God uses this method to change one form of creation to another form of creation, from a low-energy world to a high-energy world. Crucifixion, burnt offerings, resurrection, and ascension are all based upon the principles of metamorphosis.

For example, metamorphosis is self-evident in the human kingdom, animal kingdom, fish kingdom, bird kingdom, insect kingdom, and plant kingdom.

In the human and animal kingdoms, the seed is planted in the womb of the female species and needs to be fed to grow.

Chapter 18

The Full Version of Crucifixion, Burnt Offerings, Resurrection, and Ascension

THE MOST IMPORTANT POINTS THAT I want to re-emphasize for my readers to understand are crucifixion, burnt offerings, resurrection, and ascension because they are the vital keys to your Christ-like developmental stages, as well as the path and doorway to heaven. Jesus said, "I am the way, the truth and the life. Nobody cometh to the father but by Me," John 14:6.

This was the most powerful statement ever made by Jesus, and He went on to prove it to the human race on earth by giving the world a public demonstration that crucifixion, resurrection, and ascension do not mean that you are dying, but rather shifting from a low-energy being to a high-energy being. You need to transform a human being with a human consciousness to a Christ-like being with Christ consciousness to be able to live in heaven, because heaven is a high-energy world and requires a high-energy body and a high-energy consciousness. A high-energy body does not have flesh and blood. It has pure high energy. A low-energy body, your human body, has flesh and blood and low consciousness, which is human consciousness.

Then let us see how Jesus played out the principles of crucifixion, burnt offerings, resurrection, and ascension in His own personal life to attain His victory over death. As you have already read in the previous chapters, the message of Jesus starts with the awakening of the holy Christ fire in the heart, also called fire baptism of the heart. John said in the Bible, "I baptize with water unto repentance, but he that cometh after me baptizes with the Holy Ghost and with fire," Matthew 3:11. This means that Jesus has the divine spark of the holy Christ fire in His heart, and He uses it to turn on the Christ fire in the heart of others. This is where the change, or the shift, to high energy begins. It is also called the awakening, or the fire baptism of the heart.

The next step is communion, or the last supper. Jesus performed this symbolically by breaking bread and sharing wine with His apostles. The wine represents His blood (high energy), and the bread represents His Christ body, the high-energy body that everybody must have before he can enter into His kingdom, or the glory of God, the high-energy world.

Jesus made His intensions clear when He spoke metaphorically to His audience, "Unless ye drink My blood and eat My flesh, ye have no part with Me," John 6:53. The drinking of the blood means you must use meditation to connect with the universal life force, the universal Christ energy, to feed the holy Christ fire in your heart to grow, and to raise your energy and your body from low to high, to Christ body with Christ blood.

As you begin to draw from the universal Christ energy to feed the holy Christ fire in your heart, the Christ fire begins to grow bigger and brighter. A new, high-energy Christ body begins to form around it to replace your old physical body. The physical body now becomes a womb in which the seed of Christ is conceived in the heart to be born and grow. Jesus said, "Except a man be born again, he cannot see the kingdom of God," John 3:3.

In order to be born again, there must be a spiritual conception, an energy conception. The seed of Christ fire has to be planted in the womb of the heart. This is where Jesus comes in to awaken the divine spark of the holy Christ fire within the secret chamber of your heart, also called the fire baptism of the heart, that the entire Christian world has overlooked.

The Bible calls this Christ seed in the heart, the hidden man of the heart, the divine man-child, Christ in you, the hope of glory." "Greater is He who is in you than he who is in the world," 1 John 4:4. These are the developmental stages of the Christ seed in your heart.

As you continue to draw energy from the universal Christ energy to feed the Christ seed in your heart through meditation, the Christ seed finally reaches its full growth. Then the white fire core in the center of your brain opens up to fire up your brain, to connect you to the universal mind of God. The Christ fire in your heart also connects you to the universal heart of God. This completes the circuit of your development into a Christ-like being and opens up direct communication with heaven, God, or Jesus, and "Except a man be born again, he cannot see the kingdom of God," John 3:3.

Now the Christ in the womb has reached His full growth and is ready to come out, that is, to be born to enter into the Kingdom of God. "Except a man be born of water of the Holy Spirit, he cannot enter into the kingdom of God." This, then, triggers the crucifixion, resurrection, and ascension. First the crucifixion of the physical body, then the resurrection of the Christ body. In other words, the breaking of the physical body for the Christ body to come out. Then it is fit to say that the birth of Christ is the birth of your own becoming like Christ. The crucifixion of Jesus on the cross is the crucifixion of your own human body of sin, disease, death, hostility, and war. The resurrection of Christ is the resurrection of your own Christ-hood.

The final stage is the ascension of Christ, which is your ascension to heaven. All this can happen to you only if you receive fire baptism of the heart by Jesus and then use meditation to connect and draw from the universal Christ fire, or the universal life force, to feed the holy Christ fire in your heart until it reaches its full growth. Without this, you will not be able to enter into heaven, the high-energy world. Fire baptism of the heart and meditation are the two most critical things you cannot bypass, and yet, Christianity has bypassed them all. This is very sad indeed.

There are other important points that I want my readers to understand. They are crucifixion, burnt offerings, and resurrection. When Jesus Christ was crucified, His body was not left in the grave to rot. He was able to raise His physical body in addition to His Christ body. This was something that had never been done in human history on earth. The question is, how did He do it? The reason why the physical body breaks up during the crucifixion cycle is that the physical body cannot hold and withstand the high energies of the holy Christ body when it reaches its full growth. Let's look at the lightbulb as an example. The capacity of the bulb to hold high energy, or high electrical voltage, depends upon the number of filaments in the bulb. The power of the bulb is rated in wattage, as well as voltage. You cannot put high voltage and wattage electrical energy into a low voltage bulb. It will blow up or break apart. A low rated bulb cannot hold a high voltage unless it is rated a high voltage bulb through the increase of its internal filament.

The cells of our body operate on the same principles. The purpose of the cell is to convert the invisible energy of the universal Christ consciousness into physical light, and also to transmit and receive information. Jesus demonstrated this on the mount of transfiguration, when He transfigured his body to become like the sun and communicated with heaven.

Inside the cell is the DNA, the DNA is the heart of the cell just as the filament is the heart of the electric bulb.

The capacity of the cell to hold high energy depends upon the capacity inside the cell.

The DNA consists of two helix strands with a nucleic acid, according to scientists. It is also like a battery with acid water to generate electricity and has two polarities of positive and negative. The electric bulb also has two polarities of positive and negative electricity to ignite the bulb.

In order to bring high energy into the cells of the physical body we must increase the DNA strands in the cell of the body. Jesus was able to do that through prayer and meditation and assistance from heaven. He was able to increase his two helix strands of DNA into three and from to six and from six to nine and from nine to twelve.

Having done that, He was able to bring the high energy of the Christ body into twelve his physical body to resurrect it to blend with His Christ body to contact the physical world for a while after His resurrection.

Since He has increased the DNA strands of the cells of the physical body vehicle into twelve, His Christ body can now step in and out of the physical body vehicle at will, because the physical body is just a vehicle for him to wear to contact the physical world to do some unfinished work.

By this Jesus was able to conquer death and also fulfilled what was spoken in the bible. "And word was made flesh and dwelt among us."

That means Jesus was able to bring the high energy of the invisible holy Christ consciousness energy into the physical world, it became tangible and real, which otherwise would have remained invisible to us. He gave us a demonstration to follow. That death can be conquered by the use of the creative energy of the holy Christ consciousness.

The Burnt Offering

AFTER BREAKING UP the physical body for the Christ body to resurrect, the physical body will now go into what is known as the sacrificial lamb. Because your Christ body with Christ consciousness has stepped out from this physical body through resurrection and does not need the physical body anymore. Why? Because the Christ body is a glorified high energy body and consciousness and has no flesh and blood and can not stay in the low energy world and therefore must ascend into the glory of the God which is the high energy world.

If he chooses to stay in this low energy world to do some unfinished work then, the physical body must be modified, just like modifying your computer to increase its power capacity. That is to increase the two DNA strands. And then connect the high energy Christ body to the physical body to contact world to do some unfinished work or stay on earth for a while.

The physical body provides gravity for the Christ body to stay down here on earth, otherwise the Christ body will ascend or gravitate to high energy world or ascend to heaven.

Ascension was the last stage when Jesus transmuted the physical body completely with the holy Christ consciousness energy or fire. This is another form of burnt offering or a higher form of burnt offering. This then triggers the ascension process to the high energy world or heaven.

Earth

THE EARTH IS also going through the same cycle of crucifixion, burnt offering, resurrection and ascension.

At this stage the earth is at its crucifixion cycle that is why there are so many climatic changes, natural disasters, earthquakes, hurri-canes, storms, and etc. A new glorified diamond shinning plant is about to be born or resurrected as the old planetary body shell begins to break up for the new planet to resurrect.

Humanity and Christianity must also reach their crucifixion stage to move forward with the planet, but unfortunately they are way behind. They are suffering from what is known as spiritual or Christ-hood developmental delay because of their lack of understanding and application.

They do not know how to consciously use meditation to connect and draw from the universal Christ consciousness energy to feed the divine Christ on their own hearts to grow and arrive at their own Christhoods. Instead, they are so busy worshipping the physical flesh about him without drinking His blood and eating of His flesh that He spoke about metaphorically in the bible. The blood is the universal Christ consciousness energy which you must use meditation to connect and to draw to feed the Christ fire in your heart to grow and reach your Christhood and finally ascend with the planet. Because you and the planet fell spiritually as a unit, therefore you and the planet must ascend as a unit into the high energy world to join with the celestial systems. And you are spiritually behind because of your lack of understanding of spiritual things or high energy things.

What do you think about the sun? What energy runs the sun? What energy keeps the sun shinning everyday? There is an invisible energy that ignites the sun and keeps it running and shinning everyday, the same energy that you too must draw to ignite the sun in your heart to shine to fill your whole body to become the sun of God.

Wake up Christians and humanity. Wake up to the importance of meditation, because meditation is receiving from God. Without energy to from God you will not be able to make it to heaven. And this is precisely what you are missing because you pray to send energy to God to tell him what you want, but you do not meditate to receive what you want. Therefore your communication with God is complete and one way instead of two way communication.

Your Christ body is a crystallized body with a crystal liquid light substance like crystal water. This is what you need to create first, before you can go to heaven and live with Jesus. And this is what Christianity has completely overlooked, and it needs to be addressed. Heaven is a high-energy world, and you need to have a high-energy body to live there, and this is not happening in the Christian churches because of their lack of understanding and application.

They think they can bypass the crucifixion, resurrection, and ascension and go to heaven because Jesus has done it all for them.

Jesus shows the way. He is a high-energy being from heaven that comes and shows the pathway to heaven.

He showed us that crucifixion, resurrection, and ascension are the path and doorway to heaven, and again, crucifixion, resurrection, and ascension are all Christ-like developmental stages you must go through to arrive in heaven.

Chapter 19

The Nature of the Invisible Energy, or Fire of the Holy Christ Consciousness

THE INVISIBLE ENERGY OF THE holy Christ consciousness is a crystal, liquid white fire which emanates from the great central being that we call God and occupies the whole cosmic or universal space. It's like a giant energy ocean. This energy has creative consciousness, the God consciousness. As this creative energy of God consciousness travels across universal space from its source, it loses or lowers its intensity. This next energy is called Christ consciousness.

The Christ consciousness serves as a step-down to lower the higher energies of God so that it can be used by the material world comfortably without burning it. It is fit to say, the father gave birth to the Christ consciousness, the son.

"In the beginning was the word, and the word was with God," John 1:1. The word is the Christ consciousness, the son, and the God consciousness, the father. "All things were made by Him and without Him was not anything made that was made." That is, without the Christ consciousness, the Son, the world would not have come into manifestation.

"He came to His own, and His own receiveth Him not." That is, the Christ consciousness, the Son, came to the world that He had created, and the world that He had created did not accept Him. Jesus became the embodiment of Christ consciousness on earth, and He was not accepted.

This invisible energy of the holy Christ consciousness is similar to electric energy, but so many billion times more powerful than our natural electricity, much more refined and powerful. Jesus calls it the blood of life, the river of life, and a well springing from the everlasting life.

This is the spiritual blood that Jesus was referring to when He said, "Unless you drink my blood and eat my flesh, you have no part with me," John 6:53. When this invisible energy of the holy Christ consciousness is slowed down in vibration, it becomes physical, tangible matter. The great scientist Einstein's theory of relativity proved this point, "If you slow down energy, you get matter, and if you speed up matter, you get energy."

This proves my own personal point, that the universe is energy in physical expression. This was the reason why Jesus was able to draw on the invisible energies of the holy Christ consciousness to transform water into wine. The reason is that He is connected to this invisible force and you are not, because this is your spiritual fall, and Jesus comes to reconnect you back to your Christ consciousness, the savior within your heart.

This invisible energy is the food for the spirit, the soul, and the divine Christ spark within the secret chamber of your heart. It is a living water, and when you drink it, you will never thirst again. It is your source of spiritual food for your life. The average human is insensitive to it, so is the average Christian who thinks he is born again. This invisible energy is what blends matter and spirit to become one unified whole. It is the bridge that connects the heaven and earth together. The bridge is the holy Christ consciousness. "Nobody cometh to heaven but by me," the holy Christ consciousness.

If you want to go to heaven, then you must learn to drink the invisible liquid holy Christ energy to feed your soul, spirit, and the divine Christ fire within the secret chamber of your heart through meditation. This is the key to save yourself and the planet, as introduced by Jesus two thousand years ago.

The engine of an airplane needs fuel to burn to produce energy for the airplane to fly to reach its destination. Without fuel, what will the engine do? So you see, the divine Christ fire within the secret chamber of your heart depends upon the invisible energy of the holy Christ consciousness of the universe as fuel to burn and to grow in your heart and to create the Christ body with Christ consciousness, so you can live in heaven and in the celestial star systems, or the glory of God.

This invisible energy is like a giant cosmic ocean of liquid light that is flooding the whole cosmic space and universe with itself to feed and to sustain life. Any created thing that disconnects itself from it will be in a fallen state. That is the spiritual fall. This is the present state of earth and humanity. And Jesus came to reconnect us. Make no mistake, you must follow the rules of the reconnection process as demonstrated by the reconnection engineer, Jesus Christ. You cannot set up your own churches with your own reconnecting plan and say you are doing it in the name of the Lord. What if it doesn't work? The choice is yours.

Everything needs nourishment or fuel from God to stay alive. Therefore, to find God is to use meditation to connect with the divine spark of the holy Christ consciousness in the secret chamber of your heart, then the divine spark in your heart will connect you to the invisible energy of the holy Christ consciousness in the universal space to feed the Christ spark in your heart, and also to receive and interchange information of God's divine plan.

The cell phone works on the same principles. In order to communicate, the first thing is to awaken the internal power that resides in the heart of the phone, which is the battery. This will create the energy frequencies to connect with the external power in space to transmit and receive information from the other side.

In order to enter into the external kingdom of God, you must first enter into the internal kingdom of God within your heart. This is the absolute truth you cannot avoid. Think about it.

Chapter 20

Spiritual Advancement of Our Civilization

OUR CIVILIZATION WILL NOT BE able to move forward in spiritual advancement if we are not able to bring our minds in tune with our hearts through meditation and connect with the divine spark of the holy Christ consciousness to receive our personal divine direction, as well as the divine plan for earth and the entire human race.

We depend upon our heads and not our hearts to make important decisions to run our lives. We must bring the head and the heart to join together in balanced action.

The head is where the intellect resides, and the heart is where the divine spark of the holy Christ consciousness dwells. Intellectualism of the head without the intuitive direction of the Christ consciousness in the heart will lead humanity to destruction.

The Christ consciousness of the heart is all-knowing and all-powerful. This Christ God is the authority and the Creator who sets the rules of how life works in the universe.

We connect to the universal Christ consciousness from our hearts through meditation. Inside the heart is the throne room of God. Therefore, we have God's energy in ourselves already. Our responsibility is to learn how to use meditation to connect with God's energy in our hearts for divine direction in all that we do. This is our challenge. "Greater is He who is in you than he who is in the world." "Know ye that your body is the temple of God." "Christ in you, the hope of glory." The advancement of our civilization depends upon our contact with Christ God in our hearts to receive the celestial science and technology, the eternal gospel of the universe, and the great master plan for earth and humanity to implement it.

This then will establish direct open communication between the entire citizens of heaven and the entire citizens of earth.

In order for heaven to change the earth, heaven must communi-cate with earth openly, for how can you communicate with a being whose spiritual communication system is shut down? The first thing to do is to fix it. This was the reason why Jesus was sent to earth with a spiritual reconnection plan by the God parent from heaven.

His reconnection plan is to awaken the divine spark of the holy Christ fire, or consciousness, in your heart first, and then teach you how to use meditation to connect and to draw from the universal Christ consciousness energy as fuel, or the blood of Christ, to feed the holy Christ fire in your heart and establish a communication link between heaven and earth.

This awakening of the divine spark of the holy Christ consciousness in the heart is also called fire baptism of the heart. That was the reason why Jesus said, "Except a man be born again, he cannot see the kingdom of God."

Chapter 21

Jesus Came to the World to Convert the World to Christ Consciousness and Not to Himself

WE ARE NOT HERE ON the earth to convert the world to Catholicism, Islam, Buddhism, Christianity, or any other religion. We are here to awaken the Christ consciousness within the secret chamber of our hearts, because the key to enter into the kingdom of God is Christ consciousness. But how can we do this conversion? Here is where Jesus steps forward before us with the great master plan from our God parent in heaven.

Let's start with the fire baptism of the heart, the awakening of the divine spark of the holy Christ consciousness within the secret chamber of our hearts, the awakening of the sleeping Christ in our hearts. "Christ in you, the hope of glory," as written in the Bible, refers to this awakening.

Our hope of returning to the kingdom of God depends upon our own Christ in our hearts. This is the engine that has to be turned on to propel us to heaven, and Jesus came to give it a jump-start. With Christ awakened in our hearts, the divisions of the human race will be melted away. This will bring love, harmony, peace, and restore human dignity and enlightenment.

Christ consciousness will enable us to create heaven on earth and abundant life for all and to fulfill the admonition of the Lord's Prayer in the Bible. "Thy kingdom come, thy will be done, on earth as it is in heaven."

Hatred and anger will be dissolved and pain and suffering will vanish. Disease and death will cancel out. Life as we know it today will be no more. The physical body and consciousness that we possess today will be a thing of the past and will be replaced with the Christ body and Christ consciousness, a diamond-shining body with a high consciousness. This, then, will begin the Christ-like civilization on earth, a civilization where everybody uses Christ consciousness to run their lives. This is the goal of the divine plan for earth and her children from our beloved God parent and Jesus.

We have not been able to recognize Christ consciousness in our own hearts. The Christ consciousness is our main power base of our personal, eternal life. To disconnect ourselves from it means spiritual death. As our human consciousness is changing to Christ conscious-ness, we are entering into the kingdom of God within us by this change.

This is a journey of consciousness, from one state of consciousness to another state of consciousness, from the state of ignorance to the state of enlightenment, from the state of darkness to the state of light, from a low-energy human being to a high-energy, Christ-like being.

The worship of the flesh of Jesus is the greatest problem in the Christian churches today. The worship of the physical flesh of the Lord is not the goal of Jesus. The awakening of the sleeping Christ in our hearts by Jesus is the goal. The next thing that Jesus wants us to do is to focus our attention and depend upon our Christ in our own hearts for everything we do. This, then, relieves Jesus to do other things in His own personal life too.

The Christ in you is what responds to your needs from this time on. You must learn to bring your mind in tune with your heart to communicate with your Christ at all times. This is what Jesus did when He was on earth; He depended upon the Christ in His heart in everything He did. Therefore, you, too, must do the same thing.

Christianity has not been able to recognize the Christ conscious-ness as the God being in the heart of Jesus and also in their own hearts to establish connection in order to receive divine direction in everything they do. They have neglected their own Christ conscious-ness within the secret chamber of their own hearts. This is a serious problem in the Christian churches today.

They like to quote from the Bible, but they don't like to go directly to the Christ consciousness in their hearts to receive what God wants them to say in their time. You, too, must connect with your heart to receive what God wants you to say today in your time and stop memorizing and quoting and repeating the same thing again and again from the Bible as if God doesn't have anything to say today in your time.

The modern Christians have made the paper Bible a God which they worship, while the real Christ God in their own hearts, who wrote the Bible and the eternal gospel of the universe, has been neglected. You must learn to bring your mind in tune with your Christ consciousness in your hearts; this is the goal of your life. Your salvation is based upon your conscious connection with your Christ in your heart. You cannot change that to your own church programs which do not work. You must let go of your human concept of salvation and replace it with the Christ consciousness concept of salvation that requires you to learn how to be in tune with the Christ consciousness in your heart all the time. This is how Jesus made His ascension, and He expects you and me to do the same thing.

Chapter 22

The Holy Army of Jesus Christ at War on Earth by Holy Christ Command

WE ARE LEADING HUMANITY INTO the golden age of enlightenment, where Christ consciousness reigns predominant within the heart and mind of every soul on earth. This is our challenge as holy Christ warriors who form the holy army of Jesus Christ on earth.

We are here to reclaim the earth into the holy light universe. Christ consciousness is the key.

Christ consciousness is the divine spark that has to be awakened in your heart by Jesus first. You must use meditation to invite Jesus into your heart and then tell Him, "Beloved Jesus, my heart is open to you; please come sit in my heart and awaken the divine spark of the holy Christ consciousness within the secret chamber of my heart."

This is the true baptism which was spoken by John the Baptist in the Bible. He said, "I baptize with water unto repentance, but He that cometh after me baptize with the Holy Ghost and with fire," Holy Christ fire.

Chapter 23

Be Connected to the Holy Christ Fire for Your Salvation and Eternal Life

I WANT YOU TO DISCONNECT yourself from the false sense of salvation and be connected to the true sense of salvation.

The true sense of salvation is the fire baptism of the heart and the fire baptism of the head by Jesus the Christ. The fire baptism of the heart connects your heart to the universal heart of God. And the fire baptism of the head connects your head to the universal mind of Christ and God. This, then, completes the circuit for your salvation, Christ-likeness, and eternal life. This is the greatest blessing that God can bestow upon His beloved children of earth and the universe.

Fire baptism of the heart and head by Jesus gives you an energy jump-start to raise you from a low-energy being to a high-energy being, from a low-energy world to a high-energy world. The high-energy world is a heavenly world, holy light universe, celestial star systems, and holy planets and galaxies.

High-energy worlds are being inhabited by high-energy beings known as Christ-like beings with Christ consciousness similar to Jesus'. These are the holy light beings, divine beings, the saints robed in white.

As the energy grows intense, we move higher and higher to greater energy beings until we finally reach the two firstborn of creation, our Father-Mother God, and then to the great central being, the God of the holy light universe. It is through these two firstborn that we all come into existence, including the entire physical creation.

These two beings are literally our God parents, and we came from them. They represent the father and mother principles of creation, the Alpha and Omega of life and creation.

They gave birth to Jesus and to all of us; we belong to an eternal holy family. And we fell from the high-energy world to the low-energy world, then Jesus was sent to earth by our God parent to rescue us and to propel us back home to our God parent in the high-energy world, the glory of God.

The low-energy world is a world of death where the devil reigns. The concept of low- and high- energy world beings are the bases upon which the whole universal God creation rests.

Concept one:

THERE IS A dividing energy line that separates the high-energy world from the low-energy world.

Concept two:

THERE IS A great central energy being whom we call God. His energy is what occupies the whole universal space and supplies the whole creation to keep it alive and running. The sun of our solar system is an example. The sun is located at a specific position in space with light energy radiation to fill the whole surrounding space containing the planets. The energy that comes out of it is like a giant cosmic ocean of light, where everything that swims in it is connected and receives its source of energy. The energy from the sun is about so many billion volts of energy. The energy closer to the sun is greater and much more intense than the energy farther away from the sun. A planet closer to the sun receives more energy than a planet farther away from the sun. As energy travels across space, it loses its intensity. This is what we might call voltage drop.

Let us go back to the great central being (God). God is a living being whose energy fills the whole cosmic space like a giant cosmic ocean of light. He gave birth to children and created planets, star systems, galaxies, and universes and filled them with His children and said to them, "Take dominion over them." That means you are to be a caretaker and a co-creator with him to run and expand His creation, or worlds.

This great central being first gave birth to the Alpha and Omega, the masculine principle of the Godhead and the feminine principle of the Godhead. It was through these two beings that the physical creation began and gave birth to us. They are literally our God parent, our father/mother God.

We were first living in the presence of our God parent in the high-energy world as Christ-like beings before we fell into the low-energy world and lost our Christ-likeness, or Christ consciousness. We became low-energy beings with low-energy bodies and low-energy consciousness, human bodies with human consciousness.

I want you to understand that energy behaves intelligently and has consciousness. Inside the consciousness are the creative concepts that want to be expressed and need a vehicle to express themselves through. Your body is that vehicle. "Know ye not that your body is the temple of God?" God is the energy being that lives inside the temple. "Whoever defiles the temple, him shall God destroy." That is, if you contaminate your body temple, the life force energy will leave the body temple to die.

Low Energy

LIFE'S DIFFICULTIES BEGIN when the energy becomes low; this is where we experience pain, sin, disease, anger, revenge, ignorance, confusion, jealousy, hatred, resentment, hostility, war, disharmony, chaos, and destruction.

Let's say, for instance, when the energy in your mobile phone becomes low, it becomes very difficult for the cell phone to create enough frequency to communicate with the other person's cell phone. Then the only solution is to raise the energy of the cell phone by charging the cell phone. You have just brought the low energy to high energy.

High Energy

HIGH ENERGY CANCELS out low energy and restores harmony and alignment and makes everything work perfectly. Then the solution to humanity's problem is to raise the energy of the entire human race and the planet from low energy to high energy in order to restore harmony and peace and propel them to the high-energy world, the glory of God.

High energy comes to cancel out sin, death, disease, pain, suffering, hardship, ignorance, anger, hatred, hostility, resentment, wars, and destruction. And so a high-energy being named Jesus walked the earth canceling out humanity's low energy of pain, disease, death, anger, hatred, hostilities, resentment, and war. This high-energy being, Jesus, came to show humanity that the solution to our problem is to raise our energy from low to high.

He showed us that high energy cancels out low energy. With high energy, you too can cancel your own personal pain, disease, death, and the problems that beset you. Start to raise your energy now and become a master of energy. With high energy, all things are possible to you. With low energy, you will suffer pain, disease, and death, including financial problems of all kinds to keep you working like a slave and your work will become like a God that you worship.

Chapter 24

How to Conquer Death by the Power of Christ Consciousness

IT IS THE DIVINE SPARK of the holy Christ consciousness in your heart which you will use to conquer death, and not Jesus' death on the cross. It is the divine spark of the holy Christ consciousness within the secret chamber of the heart of Jesus that gave Jesus the ability to challenge death and to conquer it.

With this holy Christ fire, which is also called the holy Christ consciousness, He was able to cancel out sin, disease, and death. He was able to transfigure His body and defy the laws of gravity by walking on the sea.

He was also able to override death by raising up the dead and restoring a man's withered hand, showing the awesome powers of the holy Christ consciousness, which is the creative consciousness of God in action in the physical body of Jesus. You all must become the embodiment of holy Christ consciousness now. Without it, you have no life and no salvation, for Christ consciousness is life and life is Christ consciousness, and you cannot kill Christ consciousness.

When your Christ consciousness is awakened within the secret chamber of your heart, this begins your spiritual journey back to your celestial homeland in the holy light universe to join with the celestial star systems and to meet with your celestial brothers and sisters. All of them are Christ-like beings with Christ bodies and Christ consciousness.

Here, you will experience divine harmony and peace, divine beauty and divine love for all eternity. You will also have the opportunity to travel to see the many worlds of experiments of your Creator where you can participate in partnership with God to expand His creation.

You see, my fellow Christians, creativity is what steers the course of the universe and keeps God busy. It gives God purpose and design for being in existence; without it, life would be idle and God would have nothing to do and feel bored.

Therefore, creativity with God to expand His creation is what gives purpose for being in existence to enjoy abundant life and eternal happiness and excitement. And again, you will have the opportunity to travel to other celestial star systems to witness other Christ-like civilizations.

My friends, please open up your hearts and your minds, because you are Christ-like beings and citizens of the celestial universe, which is filled with many celestial star systems.

You are no longer earthbound, chained in the human body with human consciousness with its sin, disease, and death The Christ consciousness has removed all that from your life. It's all over now, for the Christ consciousness has taken full charge, which is God's creative consciousness in you in action. You stand victorious, one with the beloved Jesus and the universal God. It is an eternal joy beyond human description.

Chapter 25

The Principles of Life

IN ORDER TO CREATE THE Christ body with Christ consciousness, you need to apply the principles that will create it. In order to have eternal life, you need to apply the principles that will create eternal life for you. The principles that create whatever you want are what you have to draw from the universal Christ consciousness. They also have to be understood and applied.

Things don't just pop out from heaven or out of nowhere and come into existence. There is a creative energy, creative consciousness, and a creative machine of God.

And these creative elements operate on principles that you need to understand, synchronize, and enjoy. This is the bases of life. Life is energy in physical expression. Energy gives birth to consciousness and inside the consciousness are the creative concepts and ideas that want to be expressed through the physical body.

The Greatest Gift of God to You

THE GREATEST GIFT that God has given you is yourself. Therefore, give recognition to yourself, appreciate God, appreciate yourself, and give yourself respect and dignity and a deep sense of love.

You Have Spiritual Lessons to Learn on Earth

YOU HAVE SPIRITUAL lessons to learn and spiritual work to do on earth. You and all forms of life have a bond of unity to establish for the good of the planet.

Another great gift that God has given to you is the planet. Respect the planet and give a deep sense of love to your planetary home. Cherish the beloved mother earth with a heartfelt embrace, beloved children of earth.

Earth was once the most beautiful planet among the celestial star systems in our universe. It was a garden of Eden among the stars. Realize, then, that the time has come for Earth to return to its former place among the celestial star systems with you. What do you have to say about that?

Chapter 26

What the Dark Forces Have Done to the Christian Churches

WHAT THE DARK FORCES HAVE done to the Christian churches was to remove the path of personal Christlikeness from the picture.

This, then, renders the Christians powerless and puts them into a position of intellectualism and ritualism. By this, I mean they memorize, quote, and tell stories from the Bible about how wonderful and powerful Jesus and His apostles and prophets were, with no action of their own internal Christ powers or Christ consciousness involved.

A person who has made an internal connection with his Christ consciousness in the secret chamber of his heart has attained his Christlikeness and has power to put his body down and to pick it up again just like Jesus. He cannot die, and you cannot kill him. Christ consciousness cancels out death. This is the basis of your salvation.

This internal white fire of holy Christ consciousness is the true you who cannot die; therefore, by blending the physical body with this fire, the physical body also becomes immortal, saved. The Christ consciousness, then, should be the main focus in the churches to defeat the dark forces and death.

Low-energy Vision and High-energy Vision
WITH LOW ENERGY you have problems in everything. Low energy connects you to the low-energy world, including the physical world of

problems, pain, suffering, hardship, anger, disease, and death. All your visions are low-energy visions, which will also create problems for you personally, because that's what you have drawn to yourself.

It is advisable that you shift into high-energy visions. High energy cancels out low energy with all its negatives, like hate, greed, anger, suffering, pain, disease, and death.

High energy produces love, compassion, kindness, patience, wisdom, peace, enlightenment, and abundant life, including eternal life.

To shift from low-energy vision to high-energy vision, you must be given a jump-start of energy in your heart and in your mind that is the awakening of the divine spark of the holy Christ fire in your heart and mind by Jesus. This holy Christ fire energy will create the necessary high frequencies to connect you to the high-energy frequency world to draw good things into your life.

Whatever energy and vision you have in your heart and mind is what you will attract into your life and be able to express outwardly, because energy wants to express itself in matter. You are an energy being, living in a physical fleshly body.

Being in Love with Your Christ Consciousness

WHEN YOU FALL in love with your Christ consciousness, it will be forever. You will know a love far deeper than you thought possible, a love divine with the transcendent beauty of eternity. This is the true nature of Christ consciousness, which is your passport into heaven.

The Catholic Church's Rosary "Hail Mary"

"HAIL MARY, FULL of grace, the Lord is with thee; blessed art thou among women and blessed is the fruit of thy womb Jesus. Holy Mary, mother of God, pray for us sinners now and at the hour of our death. Amen."

This devotional prayer should rather be "Hail Mary, full of grace, the Lord is with thee; blessed art thou among women and blessed is the fruit of thy womb, Jesus. Holy Mary, mother of God, pray for us sons and daughters of God, now and at the hour of our victory over sin, disease, and death." Our true identities are the sons and daughters of God and not sinners.

Sin is a spiritual mistake that sons and daughters committed which brought about disease and death. This can be corrected by a divine being from God who comes to awaken the divine spark of the holy Christ fire within the secret chamber of your heart to eliminate sin, disease, and death.

Hence, Mother Mary is a Christ-like being people have chosen to call on to assist them.

When the sons and daughters of God committed sins, the divine spark of the holy Christ fire within the secret chamber of their hearts shrunk to the point of extinction. This caused them to lose contact with the rest of the universe and the glory of God, hence the spiritual fall written in the Bible.

The Catholics continue to pray "Hail Mary, pray for us sinners, now and at the hour of our death." That is what they are going to get because you get what you pray for. What you accept, you get, and you have accepted sin, disease, and death.

If they pray, "Hail Mary, pray for us sons and daughters of God now and at the hour of our victory over sin, disease, and death, amen," then sin, disease and death will be removed by the assistance of Mother Mary, Jesus, the Archangels, the God parents themselves, and all the host of heaven.

Chapter 27

A Closed Mouth

A CLOSED MOUTH NEVER GETS fed. Why? Because how can you eat while your mouth is closed? You need to open your mouth to put food in and to chew and swallow it down into your stomach.

The same is true with meditation. Meditation is a process where you open up your spiritual mouth for the universal life force, or holy Christ fire, to flow through you and into your heart to feed the divine spark to grow bigger and brighter until it fills your whole body, until you and the divine spark are blended together in one unified whole.

Chapter 28

Christian Soliders on Earth

THE AVERAGE CHRISTIAN IS LIKE a spiritual soldier on a battlefield who does not know his own power base and how to integrate with it and utilize it to defeat the enemy. Therefore, the enemy is toying with him. If a Christian does not awaken the divine spark of the holy Christ fire within his heart first before he goes to the battlefield, he is already defeated by the enemy, the devil, because the Christ in you is your personal Christ that is working or fighting through you. Your first objective is to integrate with your personal Christ within your heart, then you are a complete army.

To fight and to defeat the devil, or darkness, is to accelerate and expand the divine spark of the holy Christ light, or fire, within the secret chamber of your heart through meditation. You expand the light from your inside out; darkness cannot withstand the light.

This is how the final spiritual battle is to be fought. We don't need anymore pastors and evangelists; they are obsolete, and they use old-fashioned methods of fighting the devil. What we need are light warriors, light workers, who form the holy army of Jesus Christ using meditation to connect with the holy Christ fire within their hearts and then radiate it out to change the conditions of the world.

Or let me put it this way. Those who have been able to integrate with the personal Christ fire in their hearts, which is their power base within themselves, are the ones to go to the battlefield and fight to reclaim the earth for the glory of God. Therefore, we are calling all preachers, pastors, and evangelists to retreat from the battlefield for review, evaluation, and updating, as well as training for the final battle to reclaim the beloved mother earth for her final ascension to join with the celestial star systems with you. This is the time of awakening of the holy Christ fire within the secret chamber of every heart on the planet.

Rescue Time for Earth Children by Jesus

TO RESCUE YOU from the spiritual fall, Jesus must first anchor the divine spark of the holy Christ fire in your heart.

The Spiritual Fall

THE SPIRITUAL FALL was caused by the shrinking of the holy Christ fire in your heart due to an attack by Lucifer on the innocent godly souls on the planet earth who had never experienced this before in the history of creation. The holy Christ fire energy shrunk from high energy to low energy. Lucifer's fall was also the first in the history of creation. High energy generates high vibration, or frequency, and produces love, compassion, wisdom, kindness, peace, forgiveness, and the glory of God. And Jesus is the champion of the high energy. The low energy generates low vibrations and produces anger, hatred, revenge, disease, death, and all the negativities in the world. And Lucifer identifies with this and is its author.

Humanity at this moment is at the low-energy vibration called the spiritual fall. And in order to rescue them from the fall, a high-energy being must come from the high-energy world, or the glory of God, to awaken the holy Christ fire in their heart or to give them a jump-start to accelerate humanity's energy from a low-energy vibration to a higher-energy vibration. This was the purpose why our God parent sent Jesus to earth to introduce the fire baptism of the heart. The fire baptism of the heart is the starting point that every human being must go through to return to a high-energy being to be able to live in a high-energy world, which is heaven.

The main objective of Lucifer is to keep you from becoming a Christ-like being, (high-energy being). How does he do that? He has so many methods and these methods are barriers that are set to restrict the awakening and the growth of the holy Christ fire in your heart. The holy Christ fire in your heart is your full God power that has shrunk or has been shut down in you. This is the kingdom of God that is within you that Jesus spoke about. This is your power of eternal life that makes you a Christ-like being.

Lucifer's method is to feed the anger and hate energy of humanity to create war and hostility and remove peace from the world. Without peace and stability of the human consciousness, the holy Christ fire in the heart of humanity cannot be awakened. This is the weapon that Lucifer has been using effectively to keep the holy Christ fire out in humanity and on the planet. The holy Christ fire, or the Christ consciousness, is what Lucifer, the devil, fears the most; that's why he's called the anti-Christ. We can either embody the high energies of the holy Christ fire or the lower energies of Lucifer. The choice is ours to make. If you choose the high energy, then you must follow its rules to achieve it.

Love

FILL YOUR HEART and your mind with love and you will draw love into your life. Fill your heart and mind with Christ consciousness, and you will draw Christ Jesus and all the heavenly beings into your life.

Whatever you want in your life, you must first have it in yourself to create the magnet to draw it outwardly to you.

As you fill your heart and mind with anger and hatred, you will draw more of these things into your life. To change your life is to change what is inside your heart and in your mind; that is, your thoughts.

The thoughts you have in your mind and heart are what you will express in your daily life. What you think and say, you become.

Therefore, put love and creative thoughts into your mind and heart and express them to prosper in your life.

Chapter 29

We Have Two Worlds

THERE IS CHRIST CONSCIOUSNESS WORLD and the human consciousness world. The question is, how do we change the human consciousness world into a Christ consciousness world? Here is where the great master plan of Jesus comes into play to change this condition.

Your personal question is, how does one shift from human consciousness to Christ consciousness? The goal of life is not just to be saved, but to shift into your Christ consciousness to live eternally. Then, how do I connect and shift into my Christ consciousness within my heart?

In order to shift, you must first make the connection with the internal Christ through meditation and call to Jesus to give you the fire baptism of the heart, that is, to jump-start the holy Christ fire in your heart. Your feelings will serve as a gauge to tell you whether it is on or off. The Christ consciousness energy is what will propel you to heaven, not your doctrines and dogma. Heaven is a high-energy world and requires Christ consciousness to live there. Shifting their energy from low energy to high energy is where the Christians should focus their attention, not just on mere churchgoing on Sundays. How many Christians have achieved Christ consciousness in your church? The Christ consciousness requirement for living in heaven is what the entire Christian world has overlooked; they talk about salvation without the attainment of Christ consciousness.

Chapter 30

The Simple Great Master Plan of Jesus

LET'S SAY THAT YOU ARE thirsty, and there is a cup of water before you. What would you do? Would you dance around it and talk about it for two thousand years, or would you go and take it and drink it to quench your thirst? This is precisely what every reasonable person would do. Why would you spend so many years dancing and talking about a cup of water? If you don't take the cup of water and drink it, your thirst is going to remain with you for so many years, even thousands of years.

This is precisely what is going on today with humanity and some of the Christian churches and various religions. The thirst for spiritual water is the driving force that motivates them to go to churches and to devote their time to so many church programs and activities.

And yet, this thirst is not quenched. Why is it so? Because there is a living water, a spiritual water right before their face that Jesus spoke about. He said that whosoever drinks this living water shall never thirst again.

Then this should be your greatest concern. Ask this question, where is this living water that I cannot find? Then the divine hands of Jesus will stretch forth and show you the cup of the living water to drink. This living water is from a well springing from the everlasting life. It is also called the river of life in the Bible. These words, river of life, living water, spiritual water, are all symbolic language that are used to represent energy that is real, but invisible, to you like electricity. Who has ever seen electricity? And yet, this invisible energy occupies the universal space and is pressing hard upon your mind, body, and soul to enter in to feed you, to nourish and to quench your thirst forever. All that you need to do is to open up your mind, body, and soul for it to enter. This is done through meditation. In meditation, you are receiving energy from God. You become still and listen to the voice of God within your heart. You are now drinking spiritual water, living water which contains everything that you need for all eternity.

Then why don't you learn how to meditate first, to drink from the living fountain of God, instead of wasting your time with all kinds of church programs which disconnect you from your meditation so vital to your eternal life? You see, it takes energy to turn on the energy within your heart. This is where Jesus comes in with the fire baptism of the heart to turn on the holy Christ fire within your heart.

This is what is missing in the Christian churches today that needs to be restored. Without meditation, you cannot connect with the personal life force energy of God within your heart, as well as the universal life force energy of God.

You will struggle through life without assistance from God and Jesus because you think that your intellect and your church programs and activities are the solutions to your life. But life is God's energy in you in physical expression. And if you are not able to use meditation to connect to God to receive energy, then what will be your life? How will you be able to exist? And what type of energy are you going to use?

Now you see why meditation is so important. It is more important than even prayers, because in prayers, you are transmitting energy to God and asking or requesting His help in something that you want. In prayers you are depleting energy, and your energy begins to go down or drop, and it is through meditation that you receive energy to replenish yourself. Prayer, then, is transmitting energy, which contains your message to God, while meditation is receiving energy, which contains everything that God wants to give to us for eternal life.

Why is it necessary to meditate everyday? Again you have to ask yourself, why do you eat and drink every day? Because food and water are the fuel for your physical body to survive; without them, your physical body will cease to exist. Then you should also realize that with meditation, you connect with the universal life force energy of God to feed your soul and your spirit; without it, they will cease to exist. This was the reason why Jesus said, "Unless ye drink my blood and eat my flesh, ye have no part with me." You see, Jesus wants you to use meditation as your God-given tool to connect with your universal Christ energy to feed the Christ fire in the heart of your soul and your spirit. Otherwise, they will not be able to come to where He is or be a part of Him.

Jesus wants you and me to become like Him. But the only way we can become like Him is to use meditation to connect with the universal fountain, the universal life force, energy, the source of life, the blood Christ, and the living water to draw it into our heart.

It is the creative energy of the universal Christ fire that you need to connect with and draw into yourself and into your heart, through meditation, to recreate your body and consciousness into Christ body and Christ consciousness before you can go to where Jesus is today.

This is what Jesus wants you to do now. If you Christians don't drink this blood of Christ through meditation, you will not make it to heaven.

And yet, this is precisely what many Christians and churches have overlooked. If you cannot drink His blood (holy Christ energy) through meditation, then how do you expect Jesus to do to save you and bring you into the glory of God?

My fellow Christians, it takes God's energy to propel you to heaven, and if you cannot connect with God's energy through meditation and draw it into your body, then you are stuck on earth.

You are the one who is supposed to draw the energy into your body to accelerate yourself to heaven, not Jesus.

You are the one who is supposed to drink the blood of Christ through meditation and not Jesus Himself. He has already shown you the path to heaven.

The path to heaven is by raising your energy from low to high. Heaven is a high-energy world. High energy is pure energy of love, wisdom, and harmony, and it is the creative Christ consciousness of the universe. Low energy is anti-Christ consciousness of hatred, anger, greed, hostility, and war.

God is the main power station who supplies the whole universe with energy, similar to your main hydro-electric power station which supplies power to the whole country. If it were to break down, there would be no electrical power supply for your houses and your industries; everything would be at a standstill.

Realize then, that God, the supplier of energy for the whole universal life, should be revered and loved with all our hearts and minds, for without His energy, we are nothing.

God's free energy occupies the universal space. All that you need to do is to plug in and draw this free energy into your heart through meditation. It is called grace because it is a free energy, and you don't have to pay for it. It is like taking your car to a gas station to pump free gas into your gas tank. You must first open the gas tank and connect the hose to the tank inlet for the gas to flow into the tank.

The connection of the hose to the tank to receive free gas is what you might call meditation. In mediation, you are receiving energy from God. How can you survive if you do not know how to receive energy from God? Do you know the reason why you grow old and die? Do you know that if you don't charge your cell phone battery, it will go down and die? You see, you have the technology that is teaching you these things right before your eyes. And when your cell phone battery goes down, you plug it into an electrical receptacle to charge it to restore its depleted energy supply. Because if the energy is not restored, the cell phone will not have enough energy to create the required frequencies to be able to communicate with other cell phones.

Have you ever checked yourself to see if your personal life energy is low? If it continues to go down, then it will eventually go out. This is why we die. Therefore, to stop death on this planet, we must connect to God's energy through meditation in order to recharge ourselves to raise our energy. This will create enough frequencies so we can communicate with heaven to receive solutions to our problems.

When an electrical energy in an appliance goes out, the electrical energy merely withdraws to its source. It goes back to the source it came from. Why? Because the appliance is defective; that is, something has gone wrong in the appliance that needs to be fixed. Your body is like an appliance created by God which is being run by God's energy and it operates on God's creative principles to stay alive at all times. One of the most important principles is to use meditation to connect with the universal life force energy at all times, and if you do not maintain the body and follow its rules, the body will break down and God's energy will withdraw to its source. God's pure energy cannot live in a contaminated body. You must follow the creative rules of God for your body and meditate to connect with God's energy and draw into your heart and body at all times to stay alive forever. This is God's creative law for you and not somebody's opinion because you didn't create yourself.

If you stop meditation, it means you have disconnected and stopped drawing God's energy to feed your heart and body. And you are starving yourself spiritually. Remember, life is God's light and energy in you in physical expression. If you lose the energy, you lose the light and life and you will cease to exist. An example is your electric bulb. The electric bulb converts the invisible energy of electricity into physical light. The bulb is the physical vehicle of expression of light. Without the bulb connected to the electrical energy, the bulb would be useless. Without you being connected to God's energy through meditation, you, too, will eventually be useless.

Then it's time for you Christians and all of humanity to take your meditation seriously. If all the industrial machines and equipment are connected and plugged in to one giant electrical source by the use of these creative principles, then why can't we apply the same principles to our spiritual development on earth? Meditation is plugging into God's energy and drawing it into yourself. Jesus and God cannot do that for you; only you can do that for yourself. That is why Jesus said, "Unless ye drink my blood and eat my flesh, ye have no part with me." The blood is the universal Christ light which you must plug in and draw through meditation. The father and the mother cannot eat nor drink for the child; it is the responsibility of the child to learn how to eat and drink. It is the responsibility of humanity and the church members to learn how to draw from the fountain of the universal Christ energy into their hearts and bodies to transform themselves into Christ-like beings. This is done through meditation.

The concept of meditation should not be taken lightly in the Christian churches, because it is our connection bridge to God's energy. And without God's energy flowing into our bodies to replenish us, what would our lives be? We would be empty shells running around like zombies without God's energy in us. Turning on the Christ fire in your heart is done through meditation. Why? Because it takes energy to turn on energy. By meditating on Jesus and asking for His help, He is able to come into your heart to turn on the holy Christ fire within the secret chamber of your heart. This was His mission to earth. It is called the fire baptism of the heart by Jesus.

Today we have radio and television systems capable of transmitting information throughout the whole planet. Each and every home has a receptive unit capable of receiving information from these great transmitters. God could be likened to a great transmitter of energy which contains the creative information that wants to be expressed in His universe and our planet Earth. Every human being on the planet is a receptive unit that must be in tune with God's transmitting station to receive his allotment of energy and information to express it in his life. Being in tune is done through meditation. Meditation acts as a receptive unit to receive energy and information from God. We have disconnected ourselves from God through the spiritual fall, and we must reconnect. Meditation is what we must use to do that reconnection.

Everybody has to find his role in the scheme of creation. God has His role to play, and you have your role to play to complete the creative cycle of God.

God's role is to plant the seed of Christ consciousness energy in your heart through the beloved Jesus Christ fire baptism of the heart. The next step is to provide you with invisible universal life force energy as food and fuel to feed the Christ seed to grow and replace your dense human body and consciousness, so you can live in heaven where Jesus is.

Your role and responsibility is to use meditation to connect with God's invisible universal life force energy to feed the Christ seed in your heart and enable it to grow. Is this hard to understand? And yet, Christianity and humanity find it very difficult to understand. This has caused their Christ-like developmental delay.

God is pouring out His spirit upon all flesh today on the planet and yet, Christianity and humanity are not meditating to receive it. Why? Because meditation is receiving energy from God, and if you do not meditate, you will not be able to receive energy from God. If you do not learn how to open up your mouth, you will not be able to drink nor to eat. And this is the position of Christianity and humanity today.

They are dying, not because God wants them to die, but by their own choice.

The way to connect with the Creator is through meditation. The way to see the Creator and Jesus Christ is through meditation. The way to talk to the Creator and Jesus to receive your desire is through prayer or meditation, a two-way communication system that God has provided you to use for your victory. It is your two-edged sword to fight your way back home.

If you meditate and invite Jesus in, He will meet you in your heart. This is all that Jesus is asking you to do. Try it and see, because your heart is the altar of God and is the meeting station between God and man. Meditation is what you use to meet with God in your heart. I think by now, you have discovered how important your heart is.

And when you master meditation, you will never be alone for the rest of your life, because you have found a companion in your heart. This divine companion is a friend, a teacher, a father, and your Lord Christ. He will protect you, teach you, and guide you in all things until you finally return to your celestial home and live with Jesus forever.

I want my readers to understand the importance of meditation; if you cannot meditate, you will not be able to make it to heaven, or the high-energy world, because meditation is what you use as a bridge to connect with God's universal, invisible, life force energy and what you draw on to raise your personal energy from low to high. Low energy is humanity's problem. High energy is the solution to humanity's problem.

Come join with me and let's awaken humanity and Christianity to establish peace on earth with the high energies of Jesus Christ. Energy is the first cause of creation. It is the prime mover of creation, and high energy is pure energy. And where does this high energy come from? It comes from the great central being whom we call God.

We all are connected to this great central being's energy. And when we disconnect ourselves from His energy, we cease to receive energy from Him. And the remaining energy in our bodies continues to deplete and drop lower and lower, until it is completely out and you are dead.

Meditation is what you use to connect with this great central being's energy and draw into your heart and body. Your heart is the energy connection station that stores up your energy for your personal use. It is the engine that provides energy to run your body vehicle.

Your heart must stay connected to the main drive engine, the central heart of the main central being through meditation in the morning and in the evening. This, then, establishes the constant flow of energy into your heart and your body at all times.

As you increase your time of meditation, you also increase the amount of energy you draw into your heart and body. The energy in your heart and body begins to rise from low energy to high energy. You are now becoming a high-energy being like Jesus, a radiant being.

Today, there are so many people who say God can neither be seen nor talked to. God is hidden because we cannot see Him with our physical eyes. How can such a God be real? Everything around us came from some evolutionary process and not some God. This God essence is a myth and unreal, and it is a figment of our imagination.

God can be seen and can be talked to. It is rather we who have hidden ourselves from God by our own ignorance of who we are and what we are and our inability to connect with God in our hearts through meditation.

Once we learn meditation, we will see and hear God in our hearts. We will see and hear Jesus in our hearts, for the pure in heart shall see God, according to the Bible.

Then God and Jesus will tell you how the creation came into manifestation. Meditation is what the devil has taken away from humanity and the churches.

A person can only see and hear God by first connecting with God's energy in his heart through meditation.

In meditation, you are making an energy connection between you and God or Jesus to communicate. Meditation is the great master key to connect and to open the gate to heaven and enter to communicate with all the citizens of heaven.

Because the churches are not meditating to connect with God and heaven, they are not receiving any new spiritual information from God and heaven. They are only repeating the same information in the Bible again and again, as if God doesn't have anything to say. It is as if the Bible has replaced God. Instead of the Bible being the guideline to assist the church and humanity to connect with God through meditation, it is as if the Bible has replaced meditation, just like your cell phone, which converts the invisible electrical signal into an audible voice for the other person to hear. Why can't God do the same thing with meditation?

If we can use simple meditation to communicate with God, why don't we? Why would the church and humanity waste their time on unnecessary church programs and activities when simple meditation would bring "thy kingdom come, thy will be done, on earth as it is in heaven"?

It's God's energy passing through you which will change, or transform, you into a Christ-like being like Jesus. And the only way for God's energy to pass through you is to use meditation to connect with God's energy. Then this creative Christ energy will recreate the cells of your body to transform you into an immortal being.

Meditation is the greatest tool that God has given to His children to fight their way back to heaven. Without meditation to connect with Jesus or God's energy, we will not be able to return to heaven. Why? Because it is God's energy that will propel us to heaven, and if you cannot connect and draw this energy into your body, then there is nothing that God and Jesus can do for you.

It is you who are thirsty, therefore, it is you who must do the drinking from the water to quench your thirst. The water's job is to quench the thirst. Your job is to do the drinking. Your job is to flip the switch on the wall for the electricity to create light. God's job is to provide you the energy and the tool. Your job is to use meditation as your tool, to connect and draw God's energy into your body. It is the energy that will do the creative work in your body to change you. This God energy is what is called grace in the Bible. Free energy. All that you must do is to use meditation to connect and to draw it into your body. God and Jesus cannot drink for you. The father cannot eat nor drink for the child. The child must learn how to eat and drink. You must learn how to use meditation to drink from the spiritual fountain of God. The child must learn how to drink from the well springing from the everlasting life. And this is done through meditation. In meditation, you are opening up the mouth of your soul and spirit and body for God's energy to enter into the heart of your soul, the heart of the spirit, and the heart of the body. This brings transformation to all levels of your being. It changes your human consciousness to Christ consciousness, your human body to Christ's body. If humanity and Christians will not meditate, this transformation will not happen.

Ironically, Christians are so busy with long sermons, wild preaching, and so many church programs like concerts and other rituals that they have created barriers and disconnection from God's energy, which is so vital to their salvation. The apostles foresaw this when they said "They have a form of Godliness, but deny the power thereof."

Conclusion

THERE IS NO DOUBT THAT we live in a fallen world—a world of war, pain, disease, and death. Many religions stress that we can reach a better world after death. John Entsuah is here to tell you different.

In *Jesus' Great Master Plan to Rescue Earth and Her Children from the Spiritual Fall*, Mr. Entsuah explains how each and every one of us an attain a higher level of being today, right now. Meditation is the key that will allow each of us to connect directly to the pure energy that is God. Jesus was not sent to die for our sins; Jesus was sent to teach us how to turn on the fire within our hearts, which will enable us to use meditation to directly reach God.

This exciting new interpretation of Jesus and His ministry will teach you how to move from a low-energy state of being to a high-energy state, to live the way God has always intended that His children should live. You no longer have to live in a fallen world or live in hope of the next world. Heaven is within your grasp today.

References

1.   The Lord's Prayer, Matthew 6:9, Luke 11:2–4

2.   All have sinned and fallen short of the glory of God. Romans 3:23

14.   I baptize with water unto repentance, but He that cometh after me baptizes with the Holy Ghost and with fire. Matthew 3:11

14.   Go ye, therefore, and teach all nations. Matthew 28:19

24.   Eyes have not seen, nor ears heard the things that God has prepared for those who love Him. 1 Corinthians 2:9, Isaiah 64:4

27.   Know ye not that your body is the temple of God, and that the spirit of God dwells in you? 1 Corinthians 3:16, 17

27.   Greater is He who is in you, than he who is in the world. 1 John 4:4

47.   In the last days, I will pour out my spirit upon all flesh. Proverbs 1:23

52.   Unless ye drink my blood and eat my flesh, ye have no part with me. John 6:53

54.   Nobody cometh to the Father but by Me. John 14:6

58.   I come that ye might have life and that ye might have it more abundantly. John 10:10b

59.   I am the resurrection and the life. John 11:25

59.   Nobody cometh to the Father but by me. John 14:6b

59.   Seek ye first the kingdom of God and its righteousness, and all these things shall be added unto you. John 6:33

59.   Unless ye drink my blood and eat my flesh, ye have no part with me. John 6:53

64.   I am the resurrection and the life. John 11:25

65.   And the Word was made flesh and dwelt among us. John 1:14

65.   Be of good cheer for I have overcome the world. Matthew 16:33

66.   Behold all authority in heaven and on earth is given to me. Matthew 28:18

67.   Salvation is by faith, not by works. Ephesians 2:8

77.   Christ in you, the hope of glory. Colossians 1:27 84. Christ in you, the hope of glory. Colossians 1:27 89. Spirit person

89.   Know ye that your body is the temple of God. 1 Corinthians 3:16

104.   All have sinned and have fallen short of the glory of God. Romans 3:23

106.   For He descended below so that He might rise above all things.

106.   I am the way, the truth, and the life, nobody cometh to the Father, but by Me. John 14:6

122.   He that receiveth more light until the perfect day.

111.   Unless ye drink my blood and eat my flesh, ye can have no part with Me. John 6:53

112.   Except man be born again, ye cannot see the kingdom of God. John 3:3

112.   The divine man-child, the hidden man of the heart.

112.   Greater is He who is in you, than he who is in the world. 1 John 4:4

117.   And the Word was made flesh and dwelt among us. John 1:14

124. In the beginning was the Word, and the Word was with God. John 1:1

125. He came to His own and His own receiveth Him not. John 1:11

125. Unless ye drink my blood and eat my flesh, ye have no part with me. John 6:53

125. Einstein

129. Greater is He who is in you than he who is in the world. John 4:4

129. Know ye not that your body is the temple of God? 1 Corinthians 6:19

129. Christ in you, the hope of glory. Colossians 1:27

131. Christ in you, the hope of glory. Colossians 1:27

132. Thy kingdom come, thy will be done on earth as it is in heaven. Matthew 6:9